Entrepreneurship Is Not A Business Undertaking

RANNIE C. AGUSTIN

i

CONTENTS

ACKNOWLEDGMENTS

This book is not possible without the peoples of capitalism and neoliberalism that shaped the modern societies of mediocre intellectuals who conform to the present disorder, rat race, injustices, multiple standards of quality life, power and wealth accumulation as traditions, legitimate, legal and fair.

Credit is due to the individuals and institutions that assess me, my appearance, behaviours and qualifications---social, economic and academic, within the judgment and morality of neoliberalism (my God is my judge);

I am grateful to all the authors, editors, translators and publishers (and those who might not have acknowledge by me in references page) of the reference materials I used in this book without their permission. I also thanked Professor Susan Quin whose book "Management Basics" helped me refreshed with the basics of management principles which I used in Chapter III of this book;

To all the peoples from all walks of life whom I had relationships; their experiences, shared lives, stories, intelligence and emotions; and all that contained in this book are attributed to them;

To Her Royal Highness Princess Eugenie who inspired me to learn more about Entrepreneurship, incidental to her father's encouragement to put up my own business; as a consequence, my in-depth learnings and discoveries however, made me more reserved from business; and

To the Almighty God through my Lord Jesus Christ, and the Holy Spirit which lead me along the way.

-rani a.-

Chapter 1 Schumpeterian Entrepreneurship

The discussions about Entrepreneurship in this book basically progressed within Schumpeterian Entrepreneurship perspective and other works of Max Weber, Antonio Gramsci, psychologists like Carol Gilligan, sociologists and economists.

Entrepreneurship is a subject matter of economics which attracts many scholars, business and management practitioners and economists but remain a puzzle for lack of clarity and formal definition and methodology; and unclear function in economics.

*McCraw (in Leonard, 2007) narrated that ca*pitalist economies go up and down, as Schumpeter observed, but capitalist economics also grow (economic growth) over time, cycles notwithstanding. In the short run, there are ups and downs; but, in the long run, there is growth. Schumpeter judged Walrasian-style equilibrium analysis, which he admired, as empirically inadequate -- too irreducibly static to explain economic growth. Equilibrium analysis' passive, price-taking agents, and its implication of continual economic stagnation (opposite of economic development, poverty, poor quality of life, poor economic conditions of people, inaccessible commodities due to expensive price, etc.) were at odds with observable real-world business behaviour, and with the continual process of disruptive changes so evident in real economies. Schumpeter proposed the Entrepreneurship as an alternative solution and the Entrepreneur, an *"agent of change* "will be the executor of entrepreneurship.

Entrepreneurship however is interpreted or stereotyped as business venture, small business, career shift from employee to self-employed businessperson, and so on. It is commonly perceived as undertaking for individual financial freedom and economic well-being by taking and translating business opportunity into self-owned business enterprise.

This book provides alternative and truthful (although truth is relative) meaning of Entrepreneurship.

I presented some theoretical and philosophical syntheses of great people (Max Weber, Antonio Gramsci, Allport, Gilligan, etc.) in the field of philosophy, economics, sociology, psychology and academe which we can take as the bases of present situations and hypothetical (or vision) entrepreneurship. I presented some of their great works to support the idea and truth that culture, attitudes, economic and social systems, behaviours are outcomes of themselves.

The theory of entrepreneurship is developed as an alternative solution to unjust social and economic systems.

While others distorted the meaning of Entrepreneurship and deviate its purpose from uplifting socio-economic life of people to individual wealth accumulation and profit generating endeavours; this book at least provide a clear meaning of Entrepreneurship in economic sociology framework that combined the market and social aspects of human beings. While economic sociology demonstrates how political economy, institutions and social conventions, and social network and roles interact in a community that creates economic system; and how these sectors shaped changes within the system; and how they shaped individual values and behaviour, our concentration in this book is Entrepreneurship, a single sector, and part of the economic sociology, not solely and independent from others, that will help create change in economic system and individual values and behaviours shaped by new social convention.

I also discussed by connecting points raised by Schumpeter in his several works with unclear functions or theory of Entrepreneurship in economic development, the real Entrepreneurship and Entrepreneur and how they will solve economic stagnation or contribute to the economic development.

The Entrepreneurship however is not enough or cannot stand alone to realize its ends.

The idea of Schumpeter is for micro and macro activities and both for firms and individual members of the firms and communities to be undertaken but not an ideology neither a thought for political economy for monetary and fiscal policy and laws. It is a concrete undertaking of individuals inside the firms, and individuals and firms inside the communities.

This undertaking, as it involves firms and individuals towards the ends of Economic Development, requires management talents and skills. Thus, I presented in simple way (as much as I can to reach the understanding of industrial and commercial labourers and rural farmer-workers) the Principles of Management in Chapter 3 inclusive of the 4 Manager's Functions of Planning, Organising, Leading and Evaluation.,

The *Third Chapter* of this book covers the Management Principles which aimed to complement the entrepreneur with the necessary basic managerial skills for entrepreneurial endeavours.

1.1 Entrepreneurship Defined

Entrepreneurship is doing things that are not generally done in the ordinary course of business undertakings to be carried by an entrepreneur who is an agent of change or innovator for creative destruction.

-Joseph Schumpeter-

As we go along the 190 pages of this book, we must always remember that entrepreneurship is not a business undertaking or function.

Entrepreneurship is a function of doing things that help poor people improve their economic well-being and quality of life through individuals' and or firm's initiative and innovation. The firm's primary activity is to produce and deliver cost-efficient goods and or services needed by the people, priced accessible to all, while keeping the welfare of the firm's human resources and should be the first to have improve well-being and life.

Entrepreneurs are the ones who do the social and economic functions, and according to Schumpeter, it "*does*

5

not include all heads of firms or managers or industrialists who merely operate an established business, but only those who actually perform that function"

1.2. Entrepreneurship and Business Distinguished

Entrepreneurship undertaking differs from Business primarily in set goals and objectives. While business undertaking is aimed for profit, entrepreneurial undertaking is for the creation and achievement of success of getting things done for economic development. Any organization or company can be easily identified whether a business or entrepreneurial enterprise.

Joseph Schumpeter (1911), as he viewed Entrepreneurship, professed the objective of entrepreneurship: *"First of all, there is a dream and the will to found a private kingdom, usually, though not necessarily, also a dynasty... Then there is the will to conquer: the impulse to fight, to prove oneself superior to others, **to succeed or the sake, not of the fruits of success, but of success itself...Finally, there is the joy of creating, of getting things done, or simply of exercising one's energy and ingenuity"***

On the other hand, Milton Friedman (1962) pointed

the objective of **business** in his *Capitalism and Freedom*, *"there is one and only one social responsibility of business --- to use its resources and engage in activities designed **to increase its profits**."*

Schumpeter mentioned *"**private kingdom**"* which is also a dynasty. He was referring to private (non-government, or non- state-owned enterprises) organisations or firms, which can be operating or start-up, and can expand and grow like a dynasty but not necessary (not necessary because the objective of entrepreneurship, although capable of expanding as a dynasty, is not accumulation of profits and wealth which is the bottom-line of business expansions, but to approach specific socio-economic problems of the members of the organisation or employees of the organisation or members of the community

The Austrian economist also mentioned the *"will to conquer.., to fight, to prove oneself superior to others."* What he meant by this is the nature of the tasks facing the members (employees and potential entrepreneurs) of the kingdom (firms) to acquire or develop necessary characters and traits for such tasks (or more appropriately termed as struggles). It is not like a business conquest nor fight, however, that we usually see in the market filled with warring

7

products, services and brands competing against each other for conquest of the bigger or largest market share. This conquest and fight is inside the firms (or community, if start-ups). It is the entrepreneurship or the revolution. The revolution also known as innovation is against the *organisational structure and policies, products, process, supplies, and market (distribution systems &channels)*. This revolution and entrepreneur's economic and social functions however are organic to economic development to be enjoyed by firms and community members, as Hayek (1949) described it:

> *Correct characters and traits for 'carrying out a new plan' even if they do not have complete knowledge of the market situation; the success of everything depends upon intuition, the capacity of seeing things in a way which afterwards proves to be true. The more accurate we know the natural and social world, the more perfect our control of facts becomes, and the greater the extent, with time and progressive rationalization, within which things can be simply calculated, and indeed quickly and reliably calculated, the more the significance of this function decreases.*

Schumpeter's entrepreneur is different from businessmen which are the ones characterized by many economists, according to Krizner (1973), individuals capable of *'learning' in the market process* and to *adapt their behaviours and responses to the changes from the market's context.*

For Schumpeter, those are the individuals who conduct their businesses in a routine phase and certainly not distinctive characteristics of the entrepreneur viewed as an innovator or agent of change.

His declaration "to prove one's superiority" (which anyone can say to be inconsistent to equality or equitable objectives of entrepreneurship) is about the process or methods. Industrialisation and modernisation as early as 1910 in his academic life and as finance minister of Austria until his death in 1950 were observed by Schumpeter to be the major job displacement factor. The technological advancement affected job flows of the industry resulting to job loss or cheap labour as they compete against technology. They resulted to Economic stagnation (opposite of economic development) and it is not addressed by the economic growth or productivity increases brought by technology.

The innovation of process and methods will subordinate the technology to labour factor. Technology are invented but if not put into practice with innovation, according to Schumpeter, is irrelevant.

I can say on the other hand that technology must serve the purpose of labour sector to make the works and tasks lighter, easier, safer, and convenient along with the desired productivity. Technology must serve the interests and welfare of the labour force, never to replace them for the sake of profit.

In entrepreneurship, production process, methods and the means---human skills, technological input, supplies, machineries, land and other production factors are for the benefit of the people and never for profit.

1.3. Back to Basic Economics

There are significant differences between economic growth and development. The definitions are best adopted from Investopedia (2015) and Salmon Valley (2015), respectively.

1. **Economic Growth,** is an increase in the capacity of an economy to produce goods and services, compared from one period of time to another. Economic growth can be measured in nominal terms, which include inflation, or in real terms, which are adjusted for inflation.

   It also refers to the increase or growth of specific measures of national income, GDP which are commonly expressed in terms of a measure aggregate value-added.

2. **Economic Development,** on the other hand, is the development of economic wealth of countries, regions or communities for the **economic well-being and quality of life** of their inhabitants. It includes the literacy rates or education indices, life expectancy and poverty rates. Other countries use happiness economics, GNH or gross national happiness that includes the leisure time, environmental quality, economic assets index, freedom and social justice.

Economic growth of any specific measure, accordingly, is not a sufficient definition of economic development.

Thus, Economic Growth is not a guarantee for Economic Development. Economic Growth must be the proportional function of Economic Development.

1.4. Rewind to visualize and understand the Authentic Entrepreneurship

The word "entrepreneur" is a French coinage and the earliest writer to recognize the role of Entrepreneurship is Richard Cantillion (1680's − 1734). Cantillion's entrepreneur is someone who engages in exchanges for profit; specifically, he is someone who exercises business judgment in the face of uncertainty. This uncertainty (of future sales prices for goods on their way to final consumption) is rather carefully circumscribed, as Cantillion describes it, entrepreneurs buy at a certain price to sell again at an uncertain price, with the difference being their profit or loss (Hebert & Link, 2009).

Cantillon however, described the role of entrepreneur limited to coordinator or salesman and inspired by Frank Knight's desired for profit.

Grebel, et al, (2001) pointed to Francois Quesnay, the precursor of 'The Physiocratic thoughts', who reduced the role of the entrepreneur - instead of an industry leader - to a pure independent owner of a business, though endowed with individual energy and intelligence.

Jean-Baptiste Say (1767-1832) elevated the entrepreneur to a key figure in economic life. He made a sharp distinction between the entrepreneur and the capitalist. Say broadened the concept by putting "the entrepreneur at the core of the entire process of production and distribution. However, Hebert & Link (2009) noted that Say's entrepreneur ends up as "a superintendent and an administrator."

The works and ideas of the preceding personalities do not reconcile to our definition. Hence, let us eliminate all any other concepts before and ahead (who continually developed concepts about the subject in capitalist or business perspectives) of Joseph Schumpeter's time. Schumpeter's concept of entrepreneurship is the most acceptable and will be the major framework of our discussion in this book not to discuss much the details that Schumpeter is the most acclaimed authority about Entrepreneurship and bases for most works and researches in the development and progress of Entrepreneurship (even though with wrong perceptions and applications), are traced back and attributed to Schumpeter.

Schumpeter was born in 1883 the same year Karl Marx died. Schumpeter was four when his father died. An exile, he moved his household 23 times in his lifetime, living in five different countries. His first marriage failed. Though brilliant and widely accomplished, Schumpeter had to reinvent himself many times. He failed as a lawyer, was dismissed as president of a private Vienna bank, and, as the new Austrian republic's finance minister, lasted a mere seven months. Most damaging of all, in 1926 Schumpeter's second wife Annie died in childbirth, and the child died as well. Schumpeter's beloved mother died in the same year, a three-fold emotional wounding of Schumpeter.

Neoclassical Exclusion

Schumpeter believed that Entrepreneurship is of great importance for economic development. However, Grebel, et. al. (2001) noted that *"the existence of entrepreneurship in economic theory has almost been undetectable. Economists wonder why the entrepreneur has almost vanished in economic theory. The reason apparently is that with the introduction of entrepreneurial behaviour in eastern theory a model runs the risk to lose its consistency, and therefore the entrepreneur still remained a stranger in economic theory"*.

According to Barreto (1989), Entrepreneur has no space in neoclassical theory. He noted the disappearance of the entrepreneur in economic theory. He showed that on the advent of the modern theory of the firm, economists lost track of the entrepreneur.

1.5. Entrepreneurship as Socialist Smaller Groups

Lenin necessitated war of manoeuvre and waged victoriously in the East in 1917 to change the lives of the proletariats aimed to Marx's socialism. Lenin although victorious in military war, failed in attaining the genuine character of socialism. The character of a correct strategy for socialism by way of a contrast between the relationship of State and civil society in the two geopolitical circus is long debated by many political left movements and personalities. Trotsky theorised that the permanent character of the unions' movement is not the politicisation (union or military) of the general socio- economic- cultural conditions of a society in which the structures of national affair are organic to dominant power (instead of organic to ends of genuine socialism or social justice) and disorganised by individual affairs and incapable of becoming armed battlefields.

Trotsky's contention addressed Maoist people's

15

protracted war and other socialist strategists in European, Latin and Asian communist and socialist movements.

In contrast to other socialists and Marx's prediction of (worldwide) socialism, Schumpeter proposed socialism in smaller organisations (or can be formally termed as **market socialism**) as he saw capitalism as an *"evolutionary process."* Elliot (1980) sees the parallel analyses of Marx and Schumpeter. The process of changing comes from within, occurs discontinually, and brings qualitative changes or revolutions which fundamentally replace the old equilibrium and create radically new conditions.

The stimulus of revolution is with "in the sphere of industrial and commercial life" and Schumpeter rejected the idea of market demand.

The revolution inside the organisations is called "innovation." This "innovation" is focused on forms of industrial organizations inclusive of ownership, structure, products, processes, source of supplies, and market.

Schumpeter (1950) wrote this essential fact of capitalism is the "process" of Creative Destruction. This destruction however does not impose imminent danger or threat to economic stability as it creates new conditions at the same time. This approach is not political reflections of the miserable life of the people and should not be engaged politically but scientific to diverse socio-economic-cultural conditions of the organisations and communities.

In capitalism, Schumpeter (1961) observed, capitalist-employers are excluded and devoid of entrepreneurial functions. Thus, he professed that wages (profits) should be distributed to workers on the basis of the value of marginal product of labour. Everyone has equal access to surplus (*or profit in business term*) and "***no surpluses can accrue to employers of labour.*** "

Schumpeter's idea should be interpreted positively. It is an encouragement for capitalists (inclusive of corporate investors and independent like single owners or limited partners) to venture in entrepreneurial enterprises where they will take duties and responsibilities working with labourers inside the organizations, be compensated and have access to surplus together with the workers.

This Entrepreneurial modification of form of industrial organization or institutional structure will affect the economic behaviour and will transform and socialise the capitalist institutions.

It is the workers, not the capitalists, however, who are primarily encouraged by Schumpeter (in Kilby, 1971) to create, become entrepreneurs and own the establishment, production, sources of supplies and part of the reconstructed markets:

> *"[W]e call entrepreneurs not only those [who are] 'independent' businessmen... but all who actually fulfil the function...'dependent' employees of a company, like managers, members of boards of directors...On the other hand, our concept is narrower than the traditional one in that it does not include all heads of firms or managers or industrialists who merely operate an established business, but only those who actually perform that function"*

Entrepreneurs should be the agents of change, not the capitalists as he protested (which is still true and real situations in Philippines and other countries) the exclusive accessibility and availability of technology and credit for big and established firms and capitalists.

Large corporations however render the positions of small scale firms and its associated farmers and workers through subcontract productions and consumers' dependence on their "fetished" goods which are accessible from super, flea-market, convenient to *sari-sari* and rolling stores---obviously, an *"industrial and commercial"* (entrepreneurship) failure.

Schumpeter envisioned the entrepreneur as the agent of change or innovator and earns his profits in short term or temporal from successful innovations. Schumpeter rejected the risk-taking attribute as inherent to entrepreneurs, and risk for profit or risk for ROI are assigned to capitalists.

Businessmen and capitalists take advantage of the disinterest of economists and adopted entrepreneurship, nurtured but distorted the meaning, cause and vision of true entrepreneurship. It is now exclusively aimed for market concerns and profit and lost the original social and market-combined considerations.

Capitalists in disguise as entrepreneurs go into the market-side while workers and other economic forces including the *"unproductive"* workers remain side-lined by the market and still suffering from social injustices and misery.

Not anyone of them *"goes in between"* nor *"undertook"* the function of an agent of change with mission to carry the purpose of Entrepreneurship which is Economic Development, confront the uncertainties in the market (or eliminate the worries of the people about the economic and social aspect of human life, particularly the production dynamics that involve job security, wages, productivity and market behaviours that involve consumptions of needs, price, supply and accessibility).

From our visit to brief history to our observation or analysis of present situations, failure of generations and business and capitalist sectors to accomplish the purposes of Entrepreneurship, we can say that entrepreneurship is not a business or capitalist's undertaking. It is, in economic theory, not political, an economic theory, and methodology; or in economic sociology, a social convention for economic development. A convention where capitalist and businessmen voluntarily surrender some of their interests to the labour sector for mutual benefits, benefits extended to the communities, in contrast to political economy which confiscatory power of government is enacted for socialization or nationalization purposes of firms.

1.6. How did capitalism distort the meaning of Entrepreneurship?

I was a college instructor to Entrepreneurship in St. Paul Business and Law School in Palo, Leyte in 1997. I was limited with two (2) kinds of available entrepreneurship textbooks (of course several copies of those 2 kinds are available) in the library, Filipiniana and 1 U.S. copyright book written by an American author (at least available for our access). But the number of copies and kinds of the books with wrong information are not acceptable. I realised lately that I was giving my former students the wrong information and instruction about Entrepreneurship. We had discussed several issues and topics, case studies within business framework which was I considered misleading and we were really on the wrong context of the subject matter. I apologise to my former students. May this book reach them for re-education and knowledge updates.

In the United States, Drucker (in Bowdon, 2015) defined entrepreneur as "*one who starts his own, new and small business,*" noted that not every new small business is entrepreneurial or represents entrepreneurship. Also, not every entrepreneurial business is innovative.

21

Peter Drucker is a management "guru". For accuracy, a business management guru, a writer, professor, management consultant and self-described "social ecologist," who explored the way human beings organize themselves and interact much the way an ecologist would observe and analyse the biological world. Drucker's 39 books, along with his countless scholarly and popular articles, predicted many of the major developments of the late 20th century, including privatization and decentralization, the rise of Japan to economic world power, the decisive importance of marketing and innovation, and the emergence of the information society with its necessity of lifelong learning. In the late 1950s, Drucker coined the term "knowledge worker," and he spent the rest of his life examining an age in which an unprecedented number of people use their brains more than their backs.

*[E]ntrepreneurship is not 'natural'; it is not 'creative'. It is work...Entrepreneurial businesses treat entrepreneurship as a duty. They are disciplined about it...they work at it...they practice it...*is not about the psychology or character of entrepreneurs. It is not the mysterious 'flash of genius' so often ascribed to the wealth creator that interests him, but actions and behaviour.

Drucker (1985) added that "Entrepreneurs, by definition, shift resources from areas of low productivity and profit to areas of higher productivity and profit, the returns should be more than adequate to offset whatever risk there might be."

He observed McDonald's and according to him was doing things in a different, better way, and in the process creating new value. McDonald's was entrepreneurship *"by applying management concepts and management techniques (asking, What is "value" to the customer?), standardizing the "product," designing process and tools, and by basing training on the analysis of the work to be done and then setting the standards it required, McDonald's both drastically upgraded the yield from resources, and created a new market and a new customer. This is entrepreneurship."*

Drucker further described *"Entrepreneurship rests on a theory of economy and society [with] the major task in society - and especially in the economy - as doing something different rather than doing better what is already being done. It was intended as a manifesto and as a declaration of dissent: the entrepreneur upsets and disorganizes. As Joseph Schumpeter formulated it, his task is "creative destruction"*

23

Let us deal Drucker's definitions and descriptions one by one. Drucker is in contradiction against Schumpeter by saying that entrepreneur is the *"one who starts his own, new and small business."* Entrepreneurship is not a business undertaking as we have mentioned in the definition of Entrepreneurship and it is distinguished from business in our early discussion above.

Although Drucker is correct by saying that *"entrepreneurship is work [and]... a duty"* as we defined it as *"doing things"* but he is wrong because the work or duty is not for *"entrepreneurial business."* There is no such thing as *"entrepreneurial business"* in ideal and true sense. Drucker is somehow correct for describing the entrepreneurship is not about the psychology or character or *"personality trait"* of entrepreneurs. It is about discipline(d), work and practice. I agree (also somehow) with Drucker for I shared my experience and belief in Japanese Quality Cycles which requires training which we will discuss later in this book. While this contention is true, I also observed and experience the psychology or character of entrepreneurs. Drucker is generalizing his perspective and perception disregarding the truth in individuals differences motivations (intrinsic and extrinsic, behavioural and cognitive) and aptitudes. He described Entrepreneur as the one who increases productivity for profit which is obviously wrong in Schumpeter and Friedman's definition of Entrepreneurship and business.

Drucker's observations about McDonald's are true. I do not have any disagreement against them since I worked in it as Manager Trainee. *"It was doing things in a different, better way, and in the process creating new value…"by applying management concepts and management techniques (asking, What is "value" to the customer?), standardizing the "product," designing process and tools, and by basing training on the analysis of the work to be done and then setting the standards it required."* All of them however are in reference to competing restaurants or food chains. I can admit, McDonald's is great and can be the leading fast-food restaurant in USA but I cannot tell anyone that McDonald's is entrepreneurship. I always looked for my daily sales objectives in manager's log book and analysed and strategized the positioning and crew breaks and outs for the hourly labour cost objectives without consideration whether the crew needs more hourly income for school tuition fees or family needs, while the crew left were not also considered by me with regards to whether their over or multi-tasks in multiple stations were fair enough for them. It was the Daily Schedule prepared by the

1st assistant manager. I was a very good manager by hitting the targets at par excellence during my shifts but never an entrepreneur inside McDonald's. This scenario has clear links to both labour economics and organizational economics, and to behavioural economics. As Gibbons (2003) describe it, as Akerlof and Kranton recognize, once we contemplate identity as a complement to the standard economic model of single-person decision-making, several questions may arise. March (1994) asked, "When is decision-making governed by the standard model versus by identity?", and according to Ross (1977), *"how do others perceive our identity?* "Others may see me a disciple of Adam Smith, a neoliberal while others may perceive me as enchanted or irrational bureaucrat; or intellectual mediocre as I didn't know or did not have the knowledge about the situations of the crew who offed and who were left. I was detached from crew at first, but later on, sang and danced with crew in production area, drunk with them on day offs or after store ops, socially dated some crew and attended crew personal parties (I was in fact warned by my immediate supervisors and OC for several times for associating with crew in and off-store). An entrepreneur must experience their experience (work load, job-fit, environment) if practicable and the salaries (if sufficient for family needs) they are receiving so he or she can innovate the different aspects of the organisation for collective development.

The "innovated" products (designs and standards) and methods of McDonald's are quite impressive and state of the art, a world-class service and manufacturing company, descriptions which my perception and aesthetic sensibility can express without doubts as I experienced them with my all and full senses. However, the innovation of products and methods in entrepreneurship is not the way they are. Product innovation of Schumpeter which involves changing the old one to new, is in social perspective not in business perspective. Food and drinks can be produced or changed from costly to lesser cost, from expensive to less expensive without changing the value of the product or "destroying" unnecessary value of the products *("commodity fetishism"* is how Karl Marx described them) by creating new ones. The foods and drinks are essentials to human life. McDonald's foods and drinks however are accessible only to upper class or people with higher income. Through innovation, these products can be produced (in same standards and specs) with lesser costs for the consumers' affordable access in terms of price. Hence, poor people in poverty can eat and drink quality products (economic development is getting obvious and realistic product cycle and growth will follow this scenario and arguments including the proceeding topic on McDonald's methods and differently-abled and aged persons can be used and expounded for evidence formulation for short and long-term Entrepreneurship undertakings discussed in chapter III, Entrepreneurship Through Management, Planning topic*).*

While the method of production of McDonald's is standardized and sophisticated but , I can say, is not innovated in Entrepreneurship's meaning, innovation is a "process of combining resources in different way the business never have done," the Entrepreneurship's innovation of methods unlike McDonald's is socially-oriented and related, and not business-oriented, includes the change in facilities and equipment that can be conducive or compatible with persons with disability or differently-abled persons, and aged (who are able and voluntarily willing to work). Labour stock with continuous creation of technology will not exclude these poor human beings who are in need of economic development. This is one form of combination of technological and human resources. Changes to be made in all aspects of the organisation must benefit the users (e.g. productivity, safety, ease, complementary to human deficiency, etc.) and should never cause displacement, neither put labour as inferior in value. This is innovation.

Since Drucker did not mention any, I will discuss in Chapter III the *"innovated source of supplies"* which can help workers and the indigenous improve their economic well-being and quality of life and the "innovated *market*" or market restructuring for accessibility.

To make my discussion short, McDonald's is business not entrepreneurship.

The activities which *"drastically upgraded the yield from resources, and created a new market and a new customer"* are not entrepreneurship but obviously business.

Lastly but not the least, Drucker is wrong by describing entrepreneurship as *"a manifesto and as a declaration of dissent"* and the entrepreneur *"upsets and disorganizes."* He might not have red or understood Schumpeter in saying that the camouflaged Entrepreneurship is the *"nearest approach to medieval lordship possible to [civilised human beings]."*

Some definitions can be attributed to Ricardo Caballero (2004)'s scientific studies about "creative destruction." On the other hand his studies supported the wrong perceptions and definitions of Entrepreneurship. According to him,

"...the process of Schumpeterian

29

creative destruction (restructuring) permeates major aspects of macroeconomic growth inclusive of economic fluctuations, structural adjustment and the functioning of factor markets while at the microeconomic level, restructuring is characterized by countless decisions to create and destroy production arrangements. These decisions are often complex, involving multiple parties as well as strategic and technological considerations. The efficiency of those decisions not only depends on managerial talent but also hinges on the existence of sound institutions that provide a proper transactional framework. Failure along this dimension can have severe macroeconomic consequences once it interacts with the process of creative destruction."

These claims by Caballero are supported by his empirical evidence, empirical evidence supporting the Schumpeterian view that the process of creative destruction is a major phenomenon at the core of economic growth in market economies. The most commonly used empirical proxies for the intensity of the **process of creative destruction are those of factor reallocation** and, in particular, job flows in manufacturing. According to his studies, job creation (destruction) is the positive (negative) net employment change at the establishment level from one period to the next, while many authors have constructed more or less comparable measures of job flows for a variety of countries and episodes. Although there are important differences across them, there are some common findings. In particular, job **creation and destruction** flows are large, ongoing, and persistent. Moreover, *most job flows* **take place within** rather than between narrowly defined sectors of the economy. Given the magnitude of these flows and that they take place mostly within narrowly defined sectors, **the presumption is strong that they are an integral part of the process by which an economy upgrades its technology**.

The most closely related evidence according to Caballero to the creative destruction component is the accounts for over 50 per cent of the ten-year productivity growth in the US manufacturing sector between 1977 and 1987. Other studies of US manufacturing based on somewhat different methodologies concur with the conclusion that **reallocation** accounts for a major component of within industry productivity growth. Bartelsman, Haltwanger and Scarpetta (2004) provide

31

further evidence along these lines for a sample of 24 countries and two-digit industries over the 1990s.

Caballero presented empirical evidence on institutional impediments to creative destruction and their cost. He said *"that technological -- adjustment consumes resources...but "over" regulation and other man-made institutional impediments are also a source of depressed restructuring."* In other words *"labour market regulation hinders the process of creative destruction,"*

In Caballero et. al. (2004)'s study, this hypothesis is used in a sectoral panel for 60countries and **found that job security provisions** -- measured by variables such as grounds for dismissal protection, protection regarding dismissal, procedures, notice and severance payments, and protection of employment in the constitution -- **hamper the creative destruction process**, especially in countries where regulations are likely to been forced. **By impairing worker movements from less to more productive units, effective labour protection reduces aggregate output and slowdown economic growth.**

Caballero in his final remarks, concluded that evidence and models coincide with the process of creative destruction as an integral part of economic growth and fluctuations (Caballero, 2004, all emphases in italics and bold are mine).

Caballeros' empirical evidence and models as he claimed in his final remarks are coincidence. Thus, it is not certainly the *"process"* or the *"creative destruction" per se.*

To support Caballero's remarks on evidence and models as coincidence, not correlational phenomena with creative destruction, I will point out some wrong assumptions in the studies.

Creative destruction is not primarily for Economic Growth but certainly for Economic Development and primarily about activities in microeconomic level which aimed for organisations' and market dynamics, and communities, and individual identities (or macro and micro in economic sociology). Schumpeter did not encourage any government intervention but did not dissent against government regulations. Structural adjustments are governments' initiatives (labour, investment, fiscal and monetary policies and laws).

While some fluctuations are stimulated by governments' initiatives, some fluctuations are caused by microeconomic activities (or macro level activities in economic sociology which include firms' labour policies, sources of supplies, and market costs, etc.). Thus, I agree at this instance, with Caballero that restructuring in microeconomic level requires complex decisions involving managerial talents (Entrepreneur is not enough), strategy and technologies.

Restructuring however for Schumpeter's "creative destruction" and not for Caballero's "create and destroy" production arrangements which I already mentioned in disagreement with Drucker's description of McDonald's which involve "factor reallocation" or job flows of all human resources to labour force inclusive the differently-abled and aged persons. It is not about creation and destruction flows as the evidence demonstrated by amount or numbers and sources of flows. Destroying something in different way is what makes it creative. The armed revolution and overthrowing the government are for destruction of unfair and exploitative capitalist system but not creative.

The 50 per cent of the ten-year productivity growth in the US manufacturing sector between 1977 and 1987 never told story of economic development. In fact the poverty level of US by that time (1977 U.S. Census, 24.720 million persons, and) was increasing (to 32.221 million in 1987, and

46.180 million persons in 2010) despite of productivity growth. Growth was produced by technology, not by labour and income are not distributed to labour in the form of wages but accumulated to capital. The consumptions (industrial) are not spent by the labour (who belong to the poverty incident of 32.221 million persons) but by capitalists.

Another point is Caballero's empirical evidence on institutional impediments to creative destruction and their cost, which I can say, is leading to neo-liberalist job market. He said *"that technological -- adjustment consumes resources...but ["over"] regulation and other man-made institutional impediments are also a source of depressed restructuring.* "While Caballero is correct in technological adjustment, as Schumpeter (1911) observed that new technology *"strikes their foundation and very lives"*, labour regulations in fact can help protect the labour sector which is the main focus and beneficiary of creative destruction. Labour sector can organize, negotiate, and bargain guaranteed by the man-made regulations (laws), with the capitalists. These are the situations where and when Entrepreneurship is appropriate and timely needed.

I can say that there is no empirical evidence as of this time that can prove the creative destruction neither

Entrepreneurial success.

Thurik et.al. (2002) argued that there were significant relationships in entrepreneurship and macroeconomic performance which were supported with evidence researched from1970 to 1990 data of U.S. and Europe economic performances. The shift in policy regarding small business and entrepreneurship was coupled with a shift in economic activity from large firms to small. The most impressive and most cited is the share of the *Fortune 500*. Their employment share of large firms dropped from 20%in to 8.5% 1996 and an increase in that of small firms, indeed the share of entrepreneurship in the US labour force increased from 8% in 1972 to nearly 11% in 1988. And 23 OECD countries in the period 1974-1998 shows that across the entire sample of nations, the number of business owners grew from about 29million in 1972 to about 45 million in 1998. In spite of clear evidence of a shift toward more widespread ownership and, concurrently, of a shift toward a larger number of smaller firms, this data also reveals considerable disparity in business ownership rates across countries and over time.

Thurik, et. al. (1999) see *"small businesses as a vehicle for entrepreneurship, contributing not only to employment and social and political stability but also to innovation and competition."* But you must not be deceived by this authoritative study. Entrepreneurship is a means for economic development never an end. And nevertheless, entrepreneurship is cannot be done through small businesses.

Many of the major causes of the shift toward expanded entrepreneurship at the aggregate level, technology, level of economic development, demographic characteristics, culture and institutions argued by Wennekers, et.al. (2002) is determined by *"the opportunities (on the demand side), and the capabilities and preferences (on the supply side) that plant the seeds of nascent entrepreneurship. "*

Wennekers, et. al. further developed a framework of Entrepreneurial behaviour. According to them,

> *"[F]irm performance is influenced in three direct ways. First, the variety and competition process resulting from increased start-ups and restructuring of the economy manifests itself as an effect on firm performance. Second, in the short run, innovation often brings a premium to the innovator, in terms of higher growth of sales*

or higher business profitability (and thus also influencing firm performance). Third, economic performance at the aggregate level itself influences firm performance by creating or destroying opportunities for improved performance at the firm level."

Let us deal Thurik, et.al and Wennekers, et. al. 's arguments one by one. The evidence presented which is based from Fortune 500 is erroneously concluded due to false or wrong variables. The dependent variables and indicators are not logical variables for the Entrepreneurship study in relations to Macroeconomic performances. Growth and labour fluctuations as well as ownerships do not represent any Economic Development and data on the number (+/-) of owner-labourers. Growth does not guarantee development and ownership increases do not guarantee increase in number of entrepreneurs, and I can say, they (ownership increases) are capitalist and businessmen, and the transfer of some percentage from large to small firms of labour stocks may mean retrenchments, strategic competitions and not entrepreneurial progress. Empirical evidence to support the Entrepreneurial success should have at least two phenomena. Firstly, large firms must have employment rate increases and these employed sector must be dual in status like owners or shareholders and workers at the same time and the residents of the community where firms are operating are gradually absorbed by the firms' human resources. And secondly, the employee-shareholders/owners of the large firms must have posted positive economic development indices.

The causes of *"the shift toward expanded entrepreneurship"* is also founded on wrong perception of entrepreneurship. Entrepreneurship is not from *"demand side"* pressure but from within. The *"revolution" or innovation* should start inside the firms. The changes necessary are not from the demand side or pressure nor imposed strategy of the external self-serving-interest players. This strategy of changes coming from within protects the firms and the people from *"divide and conquer"* strategy of neoliberalism.

Wennekers, et; al. (2002) provided evidences and a framework for the correlational and causal dynamics of Entrepreneurship and Economic performances which are inconsistent with the Schumpeterian Entrepreneurship and Economic Development. In Wennekers, et. al.'s framework, firm's performance is influenced in three *direct* ways. First, by competition. Second, by innovation and third, by economic performance at the aggregate level itself influences firm performance by creating or destroying opportunities for improved performance at the firm level.

The framework formulated is founded on wrong perception of entrepreneurship, innovation and creative destruction. These are defined already in our early discussions.

Another distortion made is defined by Kirzner (1973) as *"the entrepreneur [is] someone who facilitates adjustment to change by spotting opportunities for profitable arbitrage and 'disequilibrium 'situations in the market. "*

Kirzner is wrong. The Entrepreneur is the agent of change (Schumpeter, 1912). He or she must bring change and everyone should adjust to change. No one can adjust to change if it is not yet in place. The change is not aimed for profit neither for opportunities for profit. It is aimed for economic development or spotting poor communities for economic development.

Another wrong interpretation of Entrepreneurship has been modelled as an occupational choice between self-employment and wage-employment by Lucas (1978), Evans and Jovanovic (1989), Murphy et al. (1991). Accordingly, someone will become an entrepreneur if profits and the non-pecuniary benefits from self-employment exceed wage income plus additional benefits from being in wage employment. Entrepreneurship is thus often synonymous with self-employment. Self-employment is often not by choice but by necessity, a distinction if often made in between necessity and opportunity entrepreneurs – as in for instance the Global Entrepreneurship Monitor.

It is almost the correct entrepreneurship. The correct Entrepreneurship is both by choice and by necessity dependent on situation, organisation or community, from *wage-employment to self- employment (but not exclusive to it. Entrepreneurship is for independent capitalist and businessmen as well by choice or by necessity)*. Entrepreneurship is by choice and by necessity and it is not individual but collective initiative from within the organization or community organized by the Entrepreneur. The workers by necessity will shift from employees' status to owners of the organization, process or methods of production, products and surplus. One major mistake is the cost-benefit analysis of the potential entrepreneur Lucas, Evans, Jovanovic, Murphy, et al. It is cited that one opted to become an Entrepreneur if profits and benefits exceed wage income from being a wage-earner employee.

In entrepreneurship, it is not the profit and benefits

versus wage income and benefits.

While the cost of the potential "entrepreneur" or labourer in self-employed status is costly and highly expensive with the capital requirements or outlay, in correct Entrepreneurship, the cost of a labourer in employee status is less expensive and remain the same (and will become more less) ---the labour intelligence and skills--- with the cost of a labourer--- the labour intelligence and skills--- in self-employed status.

The benefits however, differ gigantically. The benefit of a labourer in employee status is minimum wage (regulated) or contract wage (underground, free job market, and or labour abusive firms). Minimum or contract wage, both are minimal or insufficient income of the labourer to raise a family decently. The benefit of a labourer in self-employed status is not profit but still his or her wage. The advantage however, in Entrepreneurship, the labourer income or wage is to be determined by him or herself enough for his or her family's well-being and quality life equitable to others. The profit or surplus which is not part of the entrepreneur's objective, can be incidental to innovated products, methods of production, less cost input and restructured market, is equitably distributed to all workers in self-employed status.

.

Capitalists adopted not only the idea of entrepreneurship. Schumpeter, is claimed by *Barnett (2015)* as one of the architects of neoliberalism:

> *"In critical human geography, neoliberalism refers in the first instance to a family of ideas associated with the revival of economic liberalism in the mid-twentieth century. This is taken to include the school of Austrian economics associated with Ludwig von Mises, Friedrich von Hayek, and **Joseph Schumpeter**, characterised by a strong commitment to methodological individualism, an antipathy towards centralised state planning, commitment to principles of private property, and a distinctive anti-rationalist epistemology; and the so-called Chicago School of economists, also associated with Hayek, but also including leading monetarist economist Milton Friedman."*

Schumpeter was in fact, envisioned profit-free enterprises and all-surplus-for-all-workers[1] organisations (which are never have done by business undertakings), a man who did not care about ROI or return on capital or simply rejected any risks.[2]

For a more clear and concise description, Entrepreneurship is a process or method that is necessary for the system decay or for discontinuity of capitalist (greedy let me qualify it because there are capitalists which can be entrepreneurial) organisations upon creation of *socialist entrepreneurial organisations*, not libertarian nor neoliberal organisations.

I used the term *socialist entrepreneurial organisations* to ensure that the meaning will be free from misinterpretation. It is to distinguished itself from socialist organisations (particularly the nationalized companies in U.K., Russia, China, Germany, Hungary, U.S., and

---

Notes:

[1] Schumpeter (1961) *[C]apitalist-employers are excluded and devoid of entrepreneurial functions. Wages (profits) should be distributed to workers on the basis of the value of marginal product of labour. Everyone has equal access to surplus (or profit in business term) and no surpluses can accrue to employers of labour.*

[2] Schumpeter, 1950). *[I]n capitalist reality, it is not competition which counts but the competition from the new commodity, the new technology, the new source of supply, the new type of organization (the largest-scale unit of control for instance)–competition which commands a decisive cost or quality advantage and which strikes not at the margins of the profits and the outputs of the existing firms but at their foundations and their very lives.*

Philippines' GOCC's, utility companies, state universities, etc. Philippines Social Security Service which created on social democrats perspective of social welfare is operating capitalist perspective) that produce and distribute goods and services in a neoliberal perspective way which aimed for profits and not for the mere delivery of goods and services needed by, to the communities. There are several socialist organisations which accumulate profits which are abusive against labourers' wages and benefits, and consumers 'price, and which deprived the most vulnerable and marginalized sectors' access.

Schumpeter argued, as cited by Pittway & Freeman (2011, emphasis mine), that is somewhat contrary to the established thought of the time, that the important question in capitalism is *not how it supports existing structures and markets but how it creates and destroys them*. In contemporary thought 'creative destruction' is now seen as one of the crucial functions of entrepreneurial activity within an economy.

Entrepreneurship is not clear to (and "Creative Destruction" is much confusing for) most economists, scholars and businessmen. Schumpeter for unknown reasons did not use clear and specific ideas and terms.

45

Some terms are disguised, metaphors and analogies to history and other ideologies. Schumpeter, a humanitarian economist and (non-Marxist) revolutionist avoided bold statements and explanations which can be associated with revolutionary left because he did not want to antagonize or alarm the capitalists. I don't see it as an act of cowardice in contrast to the courage and boldness of Marx, Gramsci, Jesus Christ and His apostles. His decision of doing such is fair because he was most probably giving chances to, if not, he was hopeful that somehow, some capitalists would turn into Entrepreneurs.

"Medieval Lordship"

> *"[W]hat may be attained by industrial or commercial success is still the **nearest approach to medieval lordship possible to [civilised human beings]**."*

> *-Joseph A. Schumpeter-*
> *(emphasis is mine)*

What did Schumpeter mean by medieval lordship? Metaphor or analogous to his observed realities in his time or vision of the future similar to the ideal medieval society?

Let us take a short walk with Michael Curtis (1961) in the time of medieval lordship which begun in human history after the fall of Roman Empire in 467 A.D. It was a feudal system, a brutal system in history, established the social structure for lords, vassals and tenants. Lords can hold courts. They are protectors of townspeople or manoeuvre local defence for they have regimental army of vassals and can muster the population. They have the power to levy taxes, labour and materials requisitions, functions of public officials. Although, at the beginning, there was no formal act or promulgation of the lords' functions, these rules of primogeniture were enacted into a feudal law.

Vassals is a military sector whose function is political which included the fidelity to and security of king and lords, financial aid, contributions, pay homage and taxes. They are privileged to own lands in exchange or reward for performed services. They were used to buttress monarchical authority, as heavily-armed cavalry, were also employed in government routines and special missions. They are endowed with rich benefits and right to immunity.

Tenants. Tenants are the feudal workers of lords and vassal without property or fief. In 9th century however, tenants are privileged to become vassals of a lord in his territory. The opportunity to own land reached the tenants. The system however, never prevented private wars, tenants' disorders and feudal anarchy in the European region.

Is it what Schumpeter mean by his medieval lordship? Non-sense.

The *"medieval lordship"* was used by Schumpeter most probably for the description of the social and economic injustices during his time in Austria or the oppressive system employed by capitalists and businessmen during his time.

Another possible truth behind the Schumpeter's statement is his analysis and ideology parallel with Karl Marx's. Schumpeter's and Marx's works have several similarities in results from analyses about capitalism, and transition from feudalism to capitalism and both wanted to end capitalism.

Karl Marx's argued in his Grundrisse (1973) that capitalism destroys the old pre-capitalist economy (feudal system), tearing down all the barriers which hem the development of forces of production, expansions of needs, the all- sided development of production, and the exploitation and exchange of natural and mental forces. Schumpeter, hostile to capitalism like Marx, used the term *"industrial and commercial success* "and *"medieval lordship* "instead of capitalism and old pre-capitalist economy (feudalism), respectively.

The other possible equivalent of his terms is Clarke (1991)'s study about the conservative critics of liberalism which aimed to fight the evils of capitalism by turning the clock back to an idealised form of medieval society in which individualism was subordinated to the values and institutions of community, nation and religion.

Describing capitalism as the reality of "*medieval lordship* "for brutal unfair treatment of workers can be another possible truth of Schumpeter and *"can be defeated or destroyed by industrial and commercial success* (or entrepreneurship)."

Or it can be the "found private kingdom, [can be] a dynasty,"... to be conquered, with the impulse to fight, to prove labour superiority over capital and technology, *"to succeed for the sake, **not of the fruits of success, but of success itself**...Finally, **there is the joy of creating, of getting things done, or simply of exercising one's energy and ingenuity"***

Chapter 2 Different Perspective: Life, Community & Self

Different perspectives contribute to the field of Entrepreneurship through the times. Economists try to understand Entrepreneurship and the functions it plays in economic systems. Sociologists and psychologists are also seeking the concept of Entrepreneurship. It is not surprising because some people always trying to understand the world that surrounds them ---their lives, peoples around them, and their own selves. As Klimsza (2014) believes in people as they tried to understand things from history and present realities that concern all aspects of human ideals, actions and realities that caused what they are experiencing, moulded individual attitudes, constructed cultures and that shaped the societies and communities; and while examining the precise incidents and human relationships in history and realities in life, right and wrong are identified in comparison to ideals, and formed are another ideals. These people have developed ideas that gave birth to different perspectives of individual and societal alternative solutions.

"What is the right way of human behaviour in a community or organization to avoid what others had done from happening again?" or *"What is the right way of human behaviour in a community or organization to improve the present situation to what is ideal or fair?"*

2.1. Economic Perspectives

Entrepreneurship is the specific alternative economic activity (which is also a theory) proposed by Schumpeter to complement his "theory on economic development."

Let us take a tour on history and works of some economists to find some underlying principles and ingredients behind the entrepreneurial aspirations and how they synthesise ideas of what is right human behaviour in and for organisation and community development.

2.1.1. Karl Marx

Karl Marx employed a systematic analysis in his attempt to explain the harsh reality of capitalist society. In his Das Kapital, he sought a comprehensive logical description of production, consumption and finance in relation to morality and the state. He described in his *Law of Value* the capitalist production as the production of "an immense multitude of commodities." A commodity has two essential qualities first, it is useful, satisfy human need and secondly, it is sold or exchanged. All commodities are sold at their value, which the worker's wage is less than the value created during their time at work, enabling the capitalists to yield a surplus value or profit on their investments.

Marx analysed the product price system is also caused by *Commodity Fetishism* or distortion of product appearance for valuation which is a form of economic exploitation as he believed that workers are the fundamental creative source of new value. Property relations affording the right of usufruct and despotic control of the workplace to by capitalists are the devices by which the surplus value created by workers is appropriated by the capitalists.

He observed that inherent to capitalism is the incessant drive to accumulate profit and wealth by way of the capitalist receipts of an increment or "*surplus value*" higher than their initial investment, as rapidly and efficiently as possible.

As capitalists optimize profitability, labour productivity are pressured to increase, by innovating technology and production process. Labour tasks are replaced by technology resulting to massive displacement.

These unfair labour conditions are preconditions for Revolution of the workers. By socialism, concentrating workers into urban settings in large-scale production processes and linking them in a worldwide market, the agents of a potential revolutionary change are created. At the heights of capitalism, at the same time develops the preconditions for its own destruction the subjective conditions for social revolution which can only come about through the apprehension of the objective circumstances by the agents themselves and the transformation of such understanding into an effective revolutionary program.

Marx's analyses are true through the times of Schumpeter. Schumpeter observed the same scenario and also believed in capitalist system decay and must be replaced by humane system. To approach the injustices however, Schumpeter differed from Marx's social revolution of the proletariat with his Entrepreneurship inclusive of the concentrations and scopes of "*revolutionary program*" and "*innovation.*"

2.1.2. John Maynard Keynes

One of John Maynard Keynes' focuses was consumption spending. Income, according to him is the primary determinant of spending by households - if people had more income they would buy more goods and services. The relationship between income and consumption spending became a key piece of the complete macroeconomic model.

Keynes introduced the *marginal propensity to consume* (MPC), defined as the change in consumption created by an increase in income to capture the relationship between income and consumption.

This theory is true in Schumpeter's observations which prompt him to struggle for economic development through distributive justice part of entrepreneurial undertakings. He also observed, as the technology advances, technological adjustments however are made through retrenchments, downsizing, redefining tasks which made labour income less. Consumption spending by labour sector as a consequence decreases while the firms' benefit of accumulating more profit and wealth which in macroeconomic activities, are increasing and contribute sustainably to economic growth but hamper economic development. Schumpeter's "new combinations" of resources or factors of production is not met or failed to be carried by firms.

It was theorised in the Classical world that any increase in demand for workers would mean an increase in the price of workers (wage rate).Keynes disproved the Classical theory. According to him, if the supply of unemployed workers is abundant, the businesses could hire workers without any wages upward pressure. This income generation entails consumption spending for goods and services which Keynes termed as the "primary expenditure" which generated from "primary employment". This in effect, generated "secondary employment" in the production of goods and services consumed so that the final change in expenditures, employment would be multiplied by the initial consumption spending.

According to Keynes, the increased consumption spending will mean an increase in production. This will lead to increased demand for labour but the labour and capital markets where increased spending produced no upward pressure on either wages, or products' price. Price remain unchanged because workers work for the same wage and firms sell their products at the same prices and there will be an increase in output (productivity) with no increase in prices.

Anyone with sharp analytic mind can easily relate this to the contractual (5 to 6-month) employment policies of Philippines government and firms ---to stabilize labour cost. This however does not help resolve the problem of economic stagnation. Can price stabilization justify the injustices inflicted to the people for the sake of firms' and capitalists' stable profit? How can labour contract policy develop the economic well-being and quality of life of workers with 5 to 6-

month employment? Stable supply of labour will mean stable supply of profit but unstable supply of labour income will never mean economic development.

If government will aim for full employment on labour factor to obtain economic development, Keynes' assumption of price increases will occur in capitalist-driven market.

The theoretical equilibrium which contested long time ago by Schumpeter will not be effective if the morality of justification of macroeconomic policy makes poor people poorer. Schumpeter believed that Entrepreneurship can help solve the problem of economic stagnation to have development without destabilizing the price, rather from bullish behaviour as it is expected or theorized to go down (commodity price) and go up (labour price through wages and distribution of surplus) and an approach to distributive justice will be on the picture.

2.2. Social Perspectives

Let us make a review on Weber's work on Enchantment and Intellectualization of individuals, and Gramsci's Organic Intellectual and other philosophers.

2.2.1. Max Weber

Karl Emil Maximilian Weber (1864–1920), born in the Prussian city of Erfurt, is the foremost social theorist of the twentieth century, known as a principal architect of modern social science along with Karl Marx and Emil Durkheim. According to **Kim (2012)**, Weber's wide-ranging contributions gave critical impetus to the birth of new academic disciplines such as sociology as well as to the significant reorientation in economics and religious studies. His methodological writings were instrumental in establishing the self-identity of modern social science as a distinct field of inquiry; he is still claimed as the source of inspiration by empirical positivists and their hermeneutic detractors alike. More substantively, Weber's two most celebrated contributions were the "rationalization thesis," a grand meta-historical analysis of the dominance of the west in modern times, and the "Protestant Ethic thesis," a non-Marxist genealogy of modern capitalism and his "Economy and Society" (in Baier, et. al., 2001) which he analysed the economic action as a behaviour concerned with *making provisions of means for the satisfaction of desires for household (family, in non-monetary or non-capitalism) or for profit and wealth (in capitalism)*. Together, the first two-mentioned theses helped launch his reputation as one of the founding theorists of modernity (moral and ethics of communitarian versus individualism) while the latter is with emphasis on economic action (e.g. cooking & eating with or buying for husband or child) is not always have to be social (or collective).

On Weber's Intellectualization from Enchantment

Modern scientific and technological knowledge is a culmination of process, a process called *intellectualization*, the germinating grounds of human knowledge in the past, such as religion, theology, and metaphysics, were slowly pushed back to the realm of the superstitious, mystical, or simply irrational.

The process of *intellectualization, in Kim (2012)'s work, is a r*ational action or knowledge which requires some knowledge of the ideational and material circumstances in which our action is embedded, since to act rationally is to act on the basis of conscious reflection about the probable consequences of action. As such, the knowledge that underpins a rational action is of a causal nature conceived in terms of means-ends relationships, aspiring towards a systematic, logically interconnected whole. It is only in modern Western civilization, according to Weber, that this gradual process of disenchantment has reached its radical conclusion.

Rationalisation or process of intellectualization entails objectification or impersonality. Industrial capitalism reduces workers to sheer numbers in an accounting book, completely free from the fetters of tradition and non-economic considerations, and so does the market relationship vis-à-vis buyers and sellers. For another, modern law and administration also rule in strict accordance with the systematic formal codes and that is, "without regard to person." Again, Weber found the seed of objectification not in material interests alone, but in the Puritan vocational ethic and the life conduct that it inspired, which was predicated upon a disenchanted monotheistic theodicy that reduced humans to mere tools of God's providence. Ironically, for Weber, modern inward subjectivity was born once we lost any inherent value *qua*-humans and became thoroughly objectified vis-à-vis God in the course of the Reformation. Modern individuals are subjectified and objectified all at once.

Pervasive in Weber's view of rationalization is the increasing control in social and material life. Scientific and technical rationalization has greatly improved both the human capacity for a mastery over nature and institutionalized discipline *via* bureaucratic administration, legal formalism, and industrial capitalism. The calculable, disciplined control over humans was, again, an unintended consequence of the Puritan ethic of rigorous self-discipline and self-control, or what Weber called "inner-worldly asceticism." Here again, Weber saw the irony that a modern individual citizen equipped with inviolable rights was born as a part of the rational, disciplinary ethos that increasingly penetrated into every aspect of social life.

Kim Sung Ho (2012) pointed to Weber's view of rationalisation as a process taking place in disparate fields of human life with a logic of each field's own and varying directions; different fields may be rationalized in terms of different values and ends, and what is rational from one's perception may be irrational from another.

In application to observed realities and for ideals, **desired social environment** that intellectualization brought about **dramatically enhances individual freedom by helping individuals understand and navigate through the complex web of institutions in order to realize the ends of their own choice**. On the other hand, **freedom and agency are seriously curtailed** by the same force in history **when individuals are reduced to a "cog in a machine," or trapped in an "iron cage"** that intellectualisation has spawned with **irresistible efficiency and at the expense of substantive rationality** (emphases in bold are mine).

The bureaucratic "iron cage" of Weber is the modernity (technology-intensive bureaucracy efficiency) that "rationalization" has brought about in which labour interest is subordinated to technology instead of serving the labour interest by technology. These rationalizations or intellectualization processes of human beings bring us to the level of civilization where the things we do are irrational "as did the ancients when their world was not yet disenchanted of its gods and demons."

Most of us are supposed to be in disenchanted status as intellectualized or rational beings but conformity to the norms and traditions, cultural backwardness or silence developed individual attitudes which comprises the common and good sense, and makes the most among us mediocre or beasts. This will be discussed in Antonio Gramsci's works.

2.2.2. Antonio Gramsci

"All men are intellectuals, one could therefore say: but not all men in society have the function of intellectuals."

- Antonio Gramsci-

Antonio Gramsci was born in 1891, in the small town of Ales in Sardinia. He was a member of the Italian Parliament and the secretary-general of the Italian Communist Party. He was imprisoned to stop his brain from working. Despite of his poor health inside the cell, he wrote the "*Letters from Prison*" and "*Prison Notebooks*."

When one distinguishes between intellectuals and non-intellectuals, one is referring in reality only to the immediate social function of the professional category of the intellectuals, that is, one has in mind the direction in which their specific professional activity is weighted, whether towards intellectual elaboration or towards muscular-nervous effort.

The entrepreneur, according to him, by virtue of his very function, must have to some degree a certain number of qualifications of an intellectual nature although his part in society is determined not by these, but by the general social relations which specifically characterise the position of the entrepreneur within industry.

For Gramsci, **each man, finally, outside his professional activity,** carries on some form of intellectual activity, that is, he is a "philosopher", an artist, a man of taste, he participates in a particular conception of the world,

has a conscious line of moral conduct, and therefore contributes to sustain a conception of the world or **to modify it**, **that is, to bring into being new modes of thought.**

The organic intellectual therefore is performing activity outside the organization that is both intellectual and muscular-nervous effort and physical in nature developing social relations and changing the physical and social world.

The necessity of an equilibrium is determined, not by the need to fuse together the organic intellectuals with the traditional, but by the need to fuse together in a single national crucible with a unitary culture the different forms of culture imported by immigrants of differing national origins.

The problem of scarcity of intellectuals as Gramsci noted (Hoare and Smith, 1999) and *"developing new intellectuals consists of the intellectual activity that exists in everyone at a certain degree of development, modifying its relationship with the muscular-nervous effort* "towards a new equilibrium, and ensuring that the muscular-nervous effort itself, becomes the foundation of a new and integral conception of the world, in so far as it is an element of a general practical activity, which is perpetually innovating the physical and social world.

Gramsci is in disagreement with Lenin but in agreement with Marx. Lenin rejected the theory of a vanguardism which would unite intellectuals and workers, and bring socialist theory "from outside" to the proletariat— which, according to Lenin, in the course of its own, spontaneous activity can only develop "trade-union consciousness". "—let the workers carry on the economic struggle and let the Marxist intelligentsia merge with the liberals for the political 'struggle'."

During the time of Gramsci, "trade-unionism" or syndicalism in Italy was the military sector of the movement. The intellectuals are the political sector of the movement.

Intellectuals (organic) are encouraged to assimilate or integrate with the masses or workers, work with them and realize and develop new ways and thoughts in changing the physical and social world. So as in the function of Schumpeter's Entrepreneur.

History and society are characterised rather by the average run of intellectuals, and therefore by the more mediocre. Mass ideology must be the hybrid output from the combined scientific works and the great philosophical syntheses which are its real cornerstones.

Gramsci firmly believed the importance of intellectuals' attachment to the masses. The religion (Catholic Church), in his appeal, lies, in the fact that they feel very strongly the need for the doctrinal unity of the whole mass of the faithful and strive to ensure that the higher intellectual stratum does not get separated from the lower.

Gramsci's idea is more inclined to political ideology which his organic intellectual who carries a political function is of great similarity with Schumpeter's Entrepreneur with social and economic functions but both work with workers in organisations and communities.

While the organic and other intellectuals have the tendency to acquire power and more power, moving higher from the origin of status, and departing from the mass, the Entrepreneurs have the same tendencies. Thus, Gramsci encouraged the higher intellectual stratum not to separate from the lower even they are in positions of public or organizational offices.

It was Gramsci's idea of collectivization or collective transformation in opposition to capitalist individualism which he described as brutish element, like the behaviour of the

65

inmates of a zoological garden.

Collectivization in producing organization and community requires voluntarism instead of wage-labour.

There are two kinds of voluntarism---one is that theorises itself as an organic form of historico-political activity, and celebrates itself in terms which are purely and simply a transposition of the language of the individual superman to an ensemble of "supermen" and the other one is conceived as the initial moment of an organic period which must be prepared and developed; a period in which the organic collectivism, as a social bloc, will participate fully. "Vanguards," "commandos," without armies to back them up, without infantry or artillery, these too are transpositions from the language of rhetorical heroism—though vanguard and commandos as specialised functions within complex and regular organisms are quite another thing. The same distinction can be made between the notion of intellectual *élites* separated from the masses, and that of intellectuals who are conscious of being linked organically to a national-popular mass. In reality, one has to struggle against the above-mentioned degenerations, the false heroisms and pseudo-aristocracies, and stimulate the formation of homogeneous, compact social blocs, which will give birth to their own intellectuals, their own commandos, their own vanguard—who in turn will react upon those blocs in order to develop them, and not merely so as to perpetuate their gypsy domination.

2.2.3. John Rawls

"A [community] is a cooperative venture for mutual advantage…marked by a conflict as well by an identity of interests…since social cooperation makes possible a better life for all than any would have if each were to live solely by his (or her) own efforts," as John Rawls (1971)'s view collectivization against individualism.

In justice as fairness, imagine individuals in social cooperation decided to collectively act, the principles of freedom (rights and duties), and to determine the division of social benefits.

In equalities of freedom, is it right for decent working environment and wages to compete against right to profit? Or right to profit to compete against right to decent working environment and wages?

Duties of workers to employers to compete against

the duties to community? Or duties of employers to community or against the duties to workers?

In inequalities of division of social benefits, is the higher income of workers' with bigger family unfair compare to the incomes of other workers and or employers with smaller family (number of family members)?

Higher responsibilities of other workers than other workers. Employers' or community's responsibilities to workers (compensations or means for family living, health, skills, advancement, security, meeting objectives, etc.) or workers' responsibilities to employers or community (profit, security, harmony, meeting objectives, etc.).

Rawls argued that "an injustice is tolerable only when it is necessary to avoid an even greater injustice."

Inequalities according to Rawls are just or fair only if they result in particular for the least advantaged members of the community.

In Entrepreneurship, by innovating the form of a firm, some of the interests of the capitalist-owner will be surrendered to workers, the ownership and the profit will be transformed to cooperative and wages and equitable surplus distribution. This may be a form of injustice if the capitalist-owner is pressured to accept the terms of the workers to avoid closure or dissolution out of dispute. This injustice however against the capitalist is tolerable to avoid a greater injustice which the capitalism imposes against the workers and communities.

The wage and surplus may be done with distribution inequalities but this is just or fair if the advantage is in favour of the marginalized sector over the profit of the capitalist.

2.2.4. Michael Walzer

Walzer (1983) views the human society as distributive community. We come together to share, divide and exchange. We come together to produce the things (goods and services) that are shared, divide and exchanged. The production is distributed among us in a division of labour.

Everyone's place in economy, political structure, social reputations, and material possessions are all come from another people. It can be unjust or just, wrong or right.

[C]ommunal independence is the deepest meaning of self-determination and essence of communities of character, traditionally stable, ongoing associations of people with some special commitment to one another and some special sense of their common life.

Self-determination however is not absolute. It is a right usually of and exercised by smaller groups (clubs, families, organisations, or more possible community than society or state) and according to Rawls, decided by members to collectively act.

If the community is radically divided, then its territory must be divided before the right to self-determination, admission and exclusion is enjoyed.

The self-determination of foreigners or guests by an exclusive band of community members or self-determination of community members by foreigners or guests is not communal freedom but oppression.

The members of the community are free but they can't claim political territorial jurisdiction and rule over the other people with whom they share the territory, otherwise, it is a form of tyranny.

In a free market according to Friedman, persons receive exactly what each one deserves. People are rewarded in accordance with the contributions we make to one another's well-being. Walzer argued as we observe in real events of life that initiative, enterprise, innovation, hard work, prostitution of talents and skills are all sometimes rewarded, sometimes not.

Walzer clarified however that it is not right to abolish the market-oriented community when people worried or suffered from the tyranny of the marketplace. Members of communities of character should have a shift of understanding on what material things are for and how they relate to them and to other people through them.

Grabbing of things that don't come naturally is a crucial sign of tyranny.

A community's culture is the story to be told by the members to make sense of all different pieces of their social life---and justice is the doctrine that distinguishes the pieces. **Justice will make for harmony only if it first makes for separation, good fences make just communities**.

The ones who are not happy with market-oriented community must separate and form their own community, so as the ones who are not happy with social community. In economic sociology, the market oriented firm can co-exist in

71

harmony with social firm as long as the two are separated (not competing) by different assumed roles in the community and identified separate and different clientele. For example, wealthy consumers are assigned to market-oriented firms and poor consumers are for social or entrepreneurial firms. Reverse discrimination against wealthy people by entrepreneurs is fair for market-oriented firms.

In remote rural areas and countryside where money is almost unknown or forgotten, entrepreneurs can innovate the market with less monetary rewards and more calculation in natura with potential labour skills and or products produced by their indigenous members and land in exchange of products and services of the entrepreneur's firm. New social convention eliminating the existence of money is possible. Money makes people poor. Elimination of money eliminates the access barrier between the people and their needs.

Let us discuss this further in Planning Function to illustrate some ideas.

2.2.5. Psycho-sociological Perspective

Entrepreneurs as noted by Pittaway and Freeman (2011) are displaced people (e.g., political refugees, immigrants, and ethnic minorities) or socially marginalised people who have been supplanted from their familiar way of life and have somehow been forced into an entrepreneurial way of life due to their circumstances. Pittaway & Freeman found out one researcher viewed displacement as both psychological and sociological, with a rebellion against existing norms and structures being one of a few reasons for psychological displacement and linked much of his thinking on entrepreneurial behaviour back to a person's family life and their early family relationships. Although not explicitly linked it seems likely that more recent research about entrepreneurship which draws on family issues, gender, minority and immigrant entrepreneurship may owe their roots to this earlier thought. Displacement and marginalization as concepts seem to remain embedded in some of these areas of study although theories about entrepreneurship based wholly on these approaches do not seem to factor in much mainstream thought today.

2.3. Psychological Perspectives

Entrepreneurs of Schumpeter have intrinsic motivations and these are the joy of doing things, having the sense of achievement, and self-actualisation. This motivation can be cultivated through cognitive domain of a person or environmental conditioning to influence values and attitudes and affect individual behaviours.

> *"First of all, there is a dream and the will to found a private kingdom, usually, though not necessarily, also a dynasty… Then there is the will to conquer: the impulse to fight, to prove oneself superior to others, to succeed for the sake, **not of the fruits of success, but of success itself**…Finally, **there is the joy of creating, of getting things done, or simply of exercising one's energy and ingenuity."**

> *-Joseph A. Schumpeter-*

This aspect raises important implications for individual psychology---cognition and behaviour. As we recognized individual differences in people's values, attitudes and behaviours, what influences these differences?

Entrepreneurs are typically motivated and driven by intrinsic forces. Let us enquire to the works of psychologists for us to better understand what influence that make others entrepreneurs and others are not as Schumpeter concludes his theory by pointing out that individuals who are entrepreneurial may need special characteristics and skills.

A person who works in a relatively static and unchanging situation can become accustomed to his/her own abilities and experience. An Entrepreneur is working in a dynamic and ever changing situation and must cope with uncertainties in their environment and must seek to shape these uncertainties. Schumpeter (in Kilby, 1971) concludes that these are very different things: *"Carrying out a new plan and acting according to a customary one are things as different as making a road and walking along it."*

Challis & Challis (2014) described liberalism as based on individuals who are free, rational and moral. Let us see how true this is in comparison to entrepreneurship.

2.3.1. Abraham Maslow

He recognized the highest level of human motivation which is self-actualisation. A person who is happy by doing what he want is motivated by a need for self-actualization or self-fulfilment or becoming what is one capable of becoming.

An Entrepreneur is motivated by such need not by profit---to prove self-worth and capabilities, to be a successful social worker or community organizer, an Entrepreneur.

While Maslow's theory is in hierarchical order, I observed and experience the need for self-actualization can be felt by anyone along with other needs like physiological, safety, love and esteem needs, at the same time, interchangeably or simultaneously.

2.3.2. Gordon W. Allport

Gordon W. Allport (1936), a psychologist and professor, developed the **Cardinal Trait theory.** Cherry (2015) traced to Allport's work the three (3) types of traits that composed the personality: cardinal traits, central traits, and secondary traits. Cardinal traits are those that dominate personality to the point that people are famous for such traits. People with such personalities often become so known for these traits that their names are often synonymous with these qualities. Consider the origin and meaning of the following: Freudian, Machiavellian, narcissism, Don Juan, Christ-like, etc.

I have searched some prominent and great people from AJ (2015)'s list of Historical Figures that Exhibited a Cardinal Trait (of G. Allport). The following are the names of good people with good cardinal traits:

1. Abraham Lincoln for honest
2. Joan of Arc for heroic self-sacrifice

3. Mother Teresa for altruistic religious service

4. Homer for epic writer

Let me add

5. Jesus Christ, for heroic self-sacrifice.

Entrepreneur, as agent of change, with herculean tasks to accomplish driven by intrinsic motivations, also has the good traits such us altruistic character and heroic. Other traits are discussed in organizational culture in Chapter III.

While the success of Entrepreneurship can be attributed to cardinal traits of entrepreneurs and members, the common pitfalls and barriers to Entrepreneurship is also due to cardinal traits as well. This cardinal traits are the causes of Weber's failed "rationalization" or "intellectualization" to "disenchant" the "enchanted" and Gramsci failed to include the reality of Allport's theory in his analysis why during his time until now (2015), societies are consist of mediocre and not by organic intellectuals.

What is this cardinal trait that dominate differently the characters of others?

Cardinal trait however is not limited to personalities or attitudes that shape someone's values and behaviour. Allport (1936, dictionary.com), defined it as well as *"basic and dominant characteristic, such as **greed** or **ambition**, which controls the behaviour of many people."*

.   AJ (2015)'s list includes the following:

1. Ebenezer Scrooge for greed
2. Marquis de Sade for sadism
3. Machiavelli for political ruthlessness
4. Hitler for intense drive for power

2.3.3. Carol Gilligan

Sheperd (2015) the person and environment relationship, as a transition from stage to stage by conflict and dis-equilibrium, followed by equilibration, is a process of the individual assimilation to the environment and adapts it to himself. Jean Piaget also believed that moral conceptions went through such sequences, a notion that Lawrence Kohlberg at Harvard has taken much further, to a widely researched theory of the development of moral judgment.

According to Gilligan (1982), who synthesized the work of Piaget and Lawrence, the approach to morality is that individuals have certain basic rights, and that you have to respect the rights of others. And morality (1993) is an imperative to care for others. She summarized this by saying that Piaget's and Lawrence works on morality have a "justice orientation", while she synthesized that we need a morality established with "responsibility orientation".

So morality imposes restrictions on what one person can do. Let us take a look of Gilligan's' "responsibility orientation." There are **3 stages in moral development-**which she also called---**the Ethics of Care**. The first is a *selfish stage or Pre-Conventional-Person*, the second is a *belief in conventional morality*, and the third is *post-conventional*. This is a progression from selfish, to social, to principled morality.

Pre-Conventional-Person only cares for themselves in order to ensure survival. This is how everyone is as children. In this transitional phase the person's attitude is considered selfish and the person sees the connection between themselves and others.

While Conventional-Person shows more care for other people, which demonstrated in the role of mother and wife, Gilligan interpreted the situation sometimes carries on as "*to ignoring need of self.*"

In this transitional phase tensions between responsibility of caring for others and caring for self are faced. The Post-Conventional Person is in the level of acceptance of the principle of care for self and others, and shown. Some people never reach this level.

The Entrepreneur is *"post-conventional* "person who reached the level of *"principled morality."*

The Entrepreneur in contrast to capitalist and businessman is not selfish or driven by self-interests but by the responsibility of caring for self and others.

Entrepreneurship in contrast to Liberalism, individuals are not free from responsibility to care for others, rational and not enchanted rational, and have principled morality and not the "ends—justify-the-means" morality.

2.3.4. Spiritual Sources of Values and or Motivation

Religions played a big role in shaping the hegemonies of management that revolutionized social institutions and impacted economic behaviours. In Spain, human relations school was promoted by Catholic that shaped the companies' humane treatment of workers. Protestants pushed for scientific management movement in USA, UK and Germany that shaped the values and culture of individualism and self-reliance but some adopted the structural analysis of management which France and Italy differed in practice of capitalism (Dobbin, 1999)

Religious influence created not just social institutions but conventions as well, where economic conventions emerged. Religions developed intellectuals among their ranks as well as in other social institutions. Religions like political economy using coercive powers influenced education, parliaments or congress, and civil society. Her agents are the traditional intellectuals.

I will discuss here is the true Christian teachings and beliefs and not the Catholic's, neither Protestant's nor any other religions' beliefs.

Jesus Christ's teachings moulded the individual values of His disciples that constructed the Christian cultural community.

The love of neighbour or fellow human beings which include strangers, and enemies is the second great and foremost Christian teaching (Matt 22:37-40).

Christian masters or employers are responsible and accountable to Jesus Christ for their slaves or employees' well-being.

In any circumstance conflict or misunderstanding arises, Christians are bound to behave and control oneself from committing evil against evil, thus employees must do what is honourable and peaceably with all inclusive of non-Christians employers, neoliberals and should never avenge for the Almighty God will make them repay (Romans 12:17-19), if the government is inutile to discharge its divine power and authority (2Peter 2:14-14). And employers should refrain from threatening their employees.

Any grievances against each other and alternatives for settlement can be done through dialogues and mutual agreements.

And among Christian employers and employees, the following verse can be a covenant for mutual and collective good. Leaving no one---labourer or employer in disadvantaged and unjust agreement:

> *"For this is not for the ease of others and*
> *for your affliction, but by way of quality—at*
> *this present time your abundance being a*

supply to their need so that their abundance also may become a supply for your need, that there may be equality, as it is written, "he who gathered much did not have too much and he who gathered little had no lack."

-2 Corinthians 8:13-15-

(Biblehub.com)

Agustin (2009) concluded that it is not good for a Christian to be selfish and greedy. God hates such kind of people as written in the epistles of Apostle John, where he stressed that love should not be a lip service but should be with actions and in truth. And that is not limited to people whom they personally know but to strangers as well. (I John 3:17-18; III John 1:5). Every Christian is responsible to others' interests, discouraged to be in conflict but to be united as one and equal without discrimination.(I Corinthians 10:24; 12:14-25, 26).

Collectivism must be given priority than individuality but individual autonomy remains (as individual functions are used) for the common good and not for oneself.

2.3.5. Neo-liberal Political Economy

Let me introduce neoliberalism to those who do not know the strategy that give life and proof to Adam Smith's theory. This brief introduction will help you at ease of understanding why Entrepreneurship was developed by Schumpeter. What were the negative effects or evils of capitalism and businesses guided by Neoliberalism? And if you wish, this introduction will give you advantage in learning management principles and strategizing Entrepreneurship in a consistent manner.

According to Clarke (1991), neoliberalism presents itself as a doctrine based on the inexorable truths of modern economics. The foundations of modern economics, and of the ideology of neoliberalism, is Adam Smith and his work, *The Wealth of Nations*. Over the past two centuries Smith's arguments have been formalised and developed with greater examination and analytical rigour, but the fundamental assumptions underpinning neoliberalism remain those proposed by Adam Smith.

Neoliberalism is understood as an accumulation strategy aimed at restoring class power, with its seductive rhetoric of freedom, has "primarily worked as a system of justification and legitimation for whatever needed to be done to achieve this goal. So it turns out that as a 'theory', neoliberalism does not serve a terribly *practical* function in actually pursuing accumulation by dispossession at all, according to Harvey (2006) but "a benevolent mask full of wonderful-sounding words like freedom, liberty, choice, and rights, to hide the grim realities of the restoration or reconstitution of naked class power." It is a society of isolated individuals, each pursuing his own self-interest Clarke description of Smith whose economic agents are not just isolated individuals, they are property owners, and it is because they are the owners of property that some have the power, embodied in legal right, to profit from the labour of others. Smith's 'romantic' critics argued that this model ignores the most distinctive characteristics of human society – morality, religion, art and culture.

Experiences of most countries showed that the benefits of free trade flowed overwhelmingly to the more economically advanced and/or politically powerful party or the wealthiest countries such as G8. While free trade brought prosperity to the most advanced producers, less advanced producers were bankrupted, masses of people were thrown out of work and the trade of whole nations came to a standstill. This experience gave rise to demands for state protection for small producers and for the national industry of the productively less advanced countries but member-countries are prohibited from legislating contrary to GATT-WTO. For the liberal political economists, of course, periodic crises and bankruptcy were part of the healthy operation of the market, the stick that accompanied the carrots offered to the more enterprising producers. The market was not just an economic, but also a moral force, penalising the idle and incompetent and rewarding the enterprising and hard-working, for the greater good of society as a whole.

The accumulation of capital has been concentrated in the metropolitan centres of accumulation, where the living standards of the employed have certainly increased, but the inherent tendency to overproduction has led capitalism from its inception to spread its tentacles worldwide, developing the world market in the attempt to dispose of its surplus product. Indigenous producers in the peripheral regions have confronted global capitalist competition in the form of falling prices for their products, which has led to falling incomes of petty producers and the mass destruction of indigenous capitalists, while those capitalists who remain have only been able to survive by forcing down wages and intensifying labour. The accumulation of capital in the metropolitan centres has only been sustained by the pauperisation of the rest of the world, leading to a polarisation of wealth and poverty, overwork and unemployment, on a global scale.

Even in the metropolitan centres of accumulation the inherent tendencies of capitalist accumulation are undeniable. While real wages may have risen, the creation of new needs by capital has meant that the socially determined subsistence needs of the population have risen more rapidly, forcing an ever growing proportion of the population to seek work to augment the household income in the attempt to meet those needs. At the same time, a growing proportion of the population is unable to meet the ever-increasing employment demands of capital, while those in employment face the ever-growing threat of losing their jobs. Those who are not able to meet their subsistence needs through waged employment are forced into dependence on others, either other members of their families or households or through collective provision from charitable or state institutions. State provision of pension and benefit incomes to those unable to work has provided some security for the victims of capitalist accumulation, but this has not been through the beneficence of capital, it has been won through the trade union and political struggles of the working class. Moreover, the mounting cost of collective provision to counter the tendencies of capitalist accumulation has given force to the neo-liberal attempt to replace collective provision with private provision through insurance-based systems, which provides yet another channel through which capital can intensify the exploitation of the mass of the working population by intensifying and profiting from their fear of misfortune. It is routine to suggest that neoliberalism is 'imposed' on developing economies externally, through the Washington Consensus promulgated by the IMF, World Bank, and WTO.

The liberals response to their critics according to Clarke, *"the 'evils' associated with capitalism cannot be ascribed to capitalism, but represent the failures of those who are unwilling or unable to live up to its standards. Liberalism is, therefore, not so much the science of capitalism as its theology. God cannot be blamed if sinners find themselves in hell; the way to avoid hell is to live a virtuous life."*

Anyone who is a Christian can classify the liberals and neoliberalism as truth or false, good or evil in Christian perspective as I quoted and briefly explained earlier above. Liberals' thinking however, are narrowed and enslaved to their false beliefs that neoliberalism is the best among possible worlds on earth and "there is no alternative" according to UK former Prime Minister late Margaret Thatcher.

Neo-liberalism is brought by Thatcher in the UK in 80's, Reagan in the US and it is legalized and championed in the Philippines in 90's by the initiative of Senator Gloria Macapagal-Arroyo, who was charged for plunder and corruptions during her presidency.

The writings of Schumpeter clearly defined Entrepreneurship as an economic theory to be realised by an entrepreneur. It is not a business undertaking neither management. It is a strategy, a theory formulated on the foundations of different economics, sociology and psychological perspectives for Economic Development working in economic sociology framework.

The Entrepreneurship however, is not enough or cannot stand alone for Economic development to be realized. It is not a theory for political economy unlike any other theories that can be translated to monetary or fiscal policy.

The Entrepreneurship is intended for micro and macro dynamics of society which involve firms and individual members of the community to affect economic behaviours and system without any insinuation of engaging with the government or any macroeconomic players.

Chapter 3 Entrepreneurship through Management

While DiMaggio and Powell (1991) concluded that neoclassical economists contend to the theory of self-interests of individuals as primal determinants of economic behaviour, the economic sociologists believed that economic behaviour is a function of different social processes, and the economic development, according to DiMaggio, is focused on the factors that facilitate diffusion across organization or across societies.

In the past, social structures and ideologies that influence management hegemonies were explored to scrutinize such hegemonies of scientific management, human relations and structural analysis.

We have mentioned also earlier that religions played a big role in shaping the hegemonies of management that revolutionized social institutions and impacted economic behaviours.

While religious influence created not just social institutions but conventions as well, where economic conventions emerged. Religion developed intellectuals among their ranks as well as in other social institutions. Religion like political economy or neoliberalism are using coercive powers to influence education, parliaments or congress, and civil society. Her agents are the traditional intellectuals and exploit the democratic process of electing government officials; Gramsci's organic intellectuals are aimed for cultural and educational development to help change economic system. His *Ordine Nuovo* also emphasized the "scientific management of work" in relation with "scientific management" of education and training. According to Monasta (2000) *"the link between the organization of work and the organization of culture was rather envisaged by Gramsci as the new 'professional culture', the new technical and vocational preparation needed by manpower (from the skilled worker to the manager) to control and to lead industrial development, as well as the society which this development inevitably generates."*

Thus, organic intellectuals and observations of hegemony of Gramsci can help us frame the guidelines for an entrepreneur to be a genuine entrepreneur and will never be astray or misrepresented and distorted by capitalist greed.

As we supported Schumpeterian Entrepreneurship in recognition of Rawls (1979)'s contention about injustices as

91

"commissions *tolerable only when it is necessary to avoid an even greater injustice,"* and with the agreement that creative destruction (available for modern or civilized human beings) is not an imminent danger to economic stability if done in smaller scale and appropriate communities, we will provide Management Principles that will guide organic intellectuals (Gramsci) or entrepreneurs in carrying change. And the cultural hegemony or professional culture will guide the Management Principles.

Walzer (1983) suggested that if the community is radically divided, then its territory must be divided before the right to self-determination. "***Justice will make for harmony only if it first makes for separation, good fences make just communities***."

Schumpeter's entrepreneur is the same person with Gramsci (in Hoare and Smith, 1971)'s organic intellectual.

> *"Every social group, coming into existence on the original terrain of an essential function in the world of economic production, creates organically, together with itself, one or more strata of intellectuals which give it **homogeneity and an awareness** of its own function not only in the*

economic but also in the social and political fields."

You can interpret entrepreneur as organic intellectual or interchangeably in our Management discussions. This Management Principles is a prescriptive education rather than descriptive approach through dictator pedagogy than democratic pedagogy. Swallow the bitter pill and live with pride like an entrepreneur or take the sweet poison and die dishonourably like a slave-labour.

Capitalists and neoliberalism are unable or can't meet the needs for decent lives, economic well-being and quality of life desired by workers and community indigenous in poverty; the reverse of the increasing prices of commodities and other basic needs, the elimination of ever growing threats of losing jobs, the care for the aged people increasing in number.

You must agree with me by now at this far that Entrepreneurship is not a business undertaking neither a management methodology as Peter Drucker professed. Otherwise you must stop reading this for this book will not be useful for your business orientation.

Entrepreneurship is aimed for Economic development through independent and indivisible five (5) innovations: (1.) forms of organisations, (2.) Products, (3.) Methods of productions, (4.) source of supplies, and (5) markets.

It was argued that Economic Growth does not guarantee Economic Development. Economic Growth or accumulation of wealth if not justly distributed will never provide Economic Development.

It is truthful to say that Economic Development generates Economic Growth.

Entrepreneurship is not an undertaking of a person or group of persons for an organization or company alone neither for the attainment of organizational objectives like profit, competitive products and services, market leadership, etc. It is, along with the organization, for a community and community objectives.—that is Economic Development.

What is Economic Development again?

Economic Development is the development of economic wealth of countries, regions or communities for the **economic well-being and quality of life** of their inhabitants.

Wealth--- goods or services, and surplus (supplies or for final consumption) are produced not based on the demand of the market neither of the stakeholders but based within the capacity and ability of the organizations. "Doing things" in different way can generate Economic Growth and doing things without just distribution and accessibility will never have Economic Development. Therefore, Economic Development requires doing things in different way, different from business, which is just distribution and accessibility of wealth. While Economic growth, a function of available resources, is limited to the capacity, cost, price of resources and productivity, Economic development is not based on cost and price and other risks that one usually sees in business.

Our objective now is clear and that is to have Economic Development in our community. How can we attain our objective with the innovations in entrepreneurial way? We need management methodology and principles.

What is Management?

Let us define Management as a process or method of coordinating organizational resources for the attainment of set goals and objectives.

There are two (2) major and critical activities to be undertaken mentioned in management: (1) the coordination of resources and (2) attainment of goals and objectives.

The resources include human resources, technological resources and financial resources. The goals and objectives can b superordinate objectives which may include the vision, mission and goals; and subordinate objectives can be the team or departmental objectives which may include the qualitative and quantitative production of goods and human resources quantifiable welfare. We will discuss this in Planning Function topic.

Challenges Facing the Entrepreneur-Manager

While the business manager deals with employees to ensure profits, the entrepreneurial manager deals with volunteers to ensure collective and common welfare. Volunteers as human resources is a very challenging task for an entrepreneur-manager (we will discuss more about this in Organising function).

Another challenge is the different sources of funds. Business organization generally funded through the capital contribution of owners and or stockholders. Loans are extended to business organization easily and with great preference by loan and fiancé institutions. On the other hand, entrepreneurial organization are funded by entrepreneur's funding, and or donation or grants, aid by funding organisations.

Both however can generate funds through operations in the form of revenue. Entrepreneurial organization can engage in revenue oriented operation while at the start-up and growing stage. This is to avoid any abuse from members to entrepreneur or members to benefactors. Self-sufficiency is aimed by the entrepreneur and discourage the community from dependency to aid, grants or donations as much as possible.

There are other challenges confronting the entrepreneur-manager. The market –oriented community is the most challenging order to be changed by him or her. At the stage of entrepreneurial organising (different from managerial organising function), the entrepreneur has to convince, change the common and good sense of a number of community inhabitants or workers to create a "change" group to facilitate organizing. Once the organizational form is change, products, and methods, the source of supplies and the market oriented "market" has to be restructured eliminating unnecessary supply chains and distribution channels and value adding networks. This requires supply chain configurations to know exactly the what (needs of customers, required materials), where (locations, who are producing, and controlling) and how (volumes, ownership, terms of distribution, degree of independence, stages of product cycles) of the supplies to determine the most appropriate and beneficial to members, volunteers (& employees, if there are any) and final consumers, in terms of timeliness, availability, quality, accessibility (location and price). The entrepreneur-manager will eliminate the market costs by innovating the source or supplies and market by eliminating the capitalist income of contractors, middlemen, convenience store, and sari-sari store and must develop design for narrowed-span horizontal integration of sourcing supplies and products distribution, and provide income replacements for the eliminated slaves or victims of giant capitalists or neoliberalism.

Manager's Roles

The entrepreneur once in the organization he or she is the manager. The manager must adhere to the two (2) major critical activities of management. The entrepreneurial manager is:

(1.) Responsible for the resources to fit in the organization

(2.) For the realization of members' aspirations (vision, goals, and objectives).

To carry this two (2) critical activities, the entrepreneur-manager must assume roles.

The roles of Entrepreneur and Manager are categorized into three (3), namely:

1. Informational,
2. Interpersonal, and
3. Decisional.

The table on the next page illustrates the roles of an Entrepreneur and Manager which both are vital for the role execution of entrepreneurial manager:

Table 1. The Roles of an Entrepreneur and Manager

	Informational	Interpersonal	Decisional
Entrepreneur			
Role:	Transferor of Information	Catalyst and organic intellectual	Agent of change
Activity:	1. Researcher, integration with the community 2. Monitoring new technology, methodology, update knowledge, etc. 3. Inform the members through meetings, community events, announcements, coffee sessions, tambayan, barber shops, etc.	1. Elicitor and solicitor of information from community, 2. Illuminator of unclear situations and gather solutions from the community, 3. Organiser of thoughts and community.	1. Decide for the necessary actions to be taken, 2. Plan and execute with members, 3. Identify needs 4. Source for resources.
Manager:			
Role:	Monitor, Disseminator, Spokesperson	Figurehead. Leader. Liaison.	Leader. Representative. Crisis handler.
Activity	1. Assigned researchers, monitor updates through tv, magazines, news. Etc. 2. Disseminate e.g. memoranda, bulletins, meeting 3. Presentation in seminars, speeches, daily or periodic reports, etc.	1. Supervise human resources and activities, 2. Perform ceremonial activities, 3. Attend to organizational and personal concerns of human resources.	1. Plan and initiate actions, 2.Decide on issues on resources, budget, objectives, schedules, policies and standards, 3.Take corrective actions and initiate alternatives in times of crisis. 4.Resolve conflicts, 5.Adapt to changes consistent to organisational objectives.

Communication skills (mostly sourced from Intercomm, STDS) is a must for an entrepreneur to be effective in the Roles discussed above.

Communication is essential for information, negotiation, bargaining; persuasion; debating on issues without being unpleasant or abrasive to others; for presentation of ideas, organising effectively for both formal and spontaneous speeches; and for participating in group discussions. The essentials of basic communication skills of an entrepreneur-manager are the following:

1. Clear and Respectful Speaking
2. Corrective Feedback
3. Constructive Feedback
4. Active Listening
5. Nonverbal Communication

In **speaking clearly and respectfully**, you must ask the following to yourself:

Do you . . .

...strive to maintain the self-confidence and self-esteem of others when you interact with them? Or you make them feel insecure?

...**have and know your purpose** and state it? *(Communicate with a purpose. Know why you are communicating and what the goal of your communication is.)*

...**use words understandable to their level? Adapt your communication**—both your words and "nonverbal"—to the needs of your audience *and avoid using jargon or language the listener will not understand.)*

...**focus your messages** on the situation, topic, issue, or behaviour, rather than on the person?

...**ask for feedback?** *(Encourage your listeners to identify and summarize the main ideas of your message as they understand them. Also, ask questions about your message. This way you'll ensure that any misunderstandings are uncovered and cleared up.)*

While **Constructive feedback** helps a person grow, learn, improve; the destructive feedback simply undermines and devalues a person.

Communication	Destructive	Constructive
Positive (what the person does well)	• Personal • Flattery	• What the person does good, behavioural • Organisational-related or individual responsibility successes • Behaviours exemplary and contributory
Negative (what the person does poorly) **Corrective**	• You're wrong • you're stupid • personal criticism, like you're hard-headed • Hurtful and insults	• What the person does poorly according to standards, • Failures • Behaviours that that affect the work and others

Hearing and **listening** are two different activity. **Hearing** is what happens when a sound vibration hits the tympanic membrane in your ear. It is a **passive** activity. **Listening** is making sure that you attach the correct meaning to that vibration. It is an **active** effort to understand what you hear.

Listening	Hearing
• Paraphrasing the message received to signal understanding • Ask for clarity/elaboration/ explanation • Ask more information	• Nodding • Conforming • Avoiding

Nonverbal communication include touching and eye contact. **Touching** is possibly the most powerful nonverbal communication form. People communicate trust, compassion, tenderness, warmth, and other feelings through touch. Also, people differ in their willingness to touch and to be touched. Some people are "touchers" and others emit signals not to touch them. **Eye contact** is used to size up the trustworthiness of another. Counselors use this communication method as a very powerful way to gain understanding and acceptance. Speakers use eye contact to keep the audience interested.

The Managerial Skills

An entrepreneur to be a successful, he or she must have necessary skills of a manager. These are the (1) conceptual, (2) technical, and (3) humane skills.

These skills are functional to a business manager dependent on what position or where in the structure the managers is holding and sitting. The executives and senior managers are required of more conceptual skills while the managers in lower levels are needed with more technical skill. All levels are required with human skill.

The entrepreneur must have all the skills because the entrepreneurial organization is best in flat or simple structure. The entrepreneur must have **conceptual skill** to be able to imagine the better future for the organization, for the members in particular than the present status. To envision a quality life for members and beyond them, to plan and execute are from ideation is conceptual in nature.

The **humane skill** is necessary to be possessed by an entrepreneur since the main purpose of entrepreneurship is for human development in general. Human skill is the ability to work well with others or with members and volunteers.in any diverse settings and situations. An entrepreneur with this skill can balance the desire for achievement of organizational work objectives with members and volunteers personal welfare and interests. Work-life (family) balance is a good policy or protocol but requires humane skill for effective implementation. However, it is my experience and observation particularly the not-for-profit organizations, managers have more of humane skills but lack of technical skills (leading and control functions) that resulted to, most of the time, failure of meeting the objectives, inefficient operations with unnecessary efforts and expenses. These NPO's mostly turned out to be political groups courting for electoral votes from the members and communities.

The **technical skill** must be possessed by an entrepreneur to complement his or her concept. This skill is the specific knowledge or expertise on how to realize and make the concepts operant inclusive the mathematical skills. This does not involve the expertise of the specific details of every activity or tasks like for example, the details of producing rice, from ploughing to planting to milling of *palay* (to learn and doing them in appropriate and necessary times, or any production process of goods and services, is fun and will equip the entrepreneur additional knowledge to be able realize things for strategic planning, and essence of entrepreneurial and organic intellectuals to help workers realize their situations and develop new strategies and methods for their own advantage and benefits). This technical skills are more on the functions of a manager.

Management or manager's four *(4) functions are: (1) Planning, (2) Organising, (3) Leading*, and *(4) Evaluation (Control)*.

3.1. Planning Function

One secret of successful organisations is the well-defined plan. Plan provides guide for the members of the organization in which course to take and where the course is heading from the analysis of where the organization is currently standing, Plan is the start of every managerial undertaking. The plan is also the start of empowerment of the members. It helps unify the diverse perceptions and values of members to a collective leadership towards the attainment of goals and objectives. Plan boosts organization's confidence about the things (part of the plan) in the future.

1. Strategic Planning

Strategy is coined from the terms "the act of the general." If it so, there must be the act or acts of the army. Thus, allow me to define strategy in general terms of management outside the military organization as the logical courses of action at the organizational level, to be carried by all members through specific division of labour and actions guided by operational goals and objectives for the attainment of organisational set goals and objectives, short and long-terms.

Strategic Planning is the process of logical planning of alternative courses of action at the organizational level, with identification of all necessary and available resources, and assessment of the environment for the practicability of such courses of action, for the attainment of organizational set goals and objectives.

There are organizational objectives which are superordinate; and operational objectives which are subordinate.

A businessman or capitalist has superordinate objective for his or her organization like *"To be the leading producer of quality farm products at most affordable price, (Mission or goals)...quality for the satisfaction of our customers and profits for our investors and stockholders,"*

An entrepreneur however differs from businessman by setting organisational objectives which is focused on people and not on profit.

Table 2 shows examples of superordinate (organizational) objective and subordinate (operational) objectives:

Table 2. Examples of Organisational and Operational Objectives

Vision & Objectives	
Organisational	Operational
To be the leading producer and supplier of quality FARM PRODUCTS in the community of Sta. Rosa, accessible to all members, produced by our happy volunteers who enjoy our resources, wealth and surplus equitably.	1. Toproduce 1 million kgs. Of assorted quality and fresh meat and poultry for year 1; 2. To produce with zero waste; 3. To produce on time.

Another good example of superordinate goal is (Culture & Mission) *"Victoria Helena's Amazons* (fictitious organisation name) *is driven by our belief that women are important active agents of change as men for community development through empowerment."* This however sounds political and very vulnerable to misinterpretation that will cause big problems to the entrepreneur-manager and divisions among members in decision-making in which course to take if confronted by different complex situations or decisions which involve conflict of interests, ethical and moral aspects of individual members.

This kind of organisational culture and mission statements must be defined in set organizational Goals like the following examples:

1. We develop and provide maternal medical services to mothers;

2. We provide life-skills seminars and empowerment trainings for mothers to help them informed and equipped with necessary skills and taking care their healthy babies;

3. We help provide decent shelters for families to keep mothers and babies healthy;

4. We provide opportunities for women to fulfil, complete and realize their dreams which are forgotten and lost upon their untimely marriage and or bearing children; and

5. We help provide children development and care centre to give mothers time for themselves and other works.

These goals make the organizational culture and mission clear and give the beneficiaries and members the visuals about them, and the idea of how they can become agents of change.

These goals however are not enough to make effect the goals and much less the cultural hegemony and mission if these mothers and women are busy, worried and or without peace of mind or psychologically and emotionally disturbed by never ending and cyclic poverty with images of their malnourished and sick children roaming inside their minds during bed times. Jobless husbands (side-lined by the qualifications of neo-liberal job markets)' surviving economic provisions (from "extortions", borrowings, indecent free-lance one-day contractual work, petty crimes, etc.) single mothers' discriminated income, meagre and indecent wages of husbands cannot suffice their family needs and pull these women away from their active involvement. So let us add another goal to address that critical issue:

6. We will employ women to be our volunteers working for our mission and goals and compensate sufficiently for their own personal and family needs.

It must be learned that vision, mission, culture, philosophy, etc., should be broken into simpler general goals and objectives---organisational and operational objectives.

1.1. Organisational Objectives

These objectives are superordinate aimed for the attainment of vision, mission, culture, etc. They may be the following which logically address the examples given in our Planning Function, the farm and or the Victoria Helena's Amazons:

i.   Eco-Efficiency
ii. Quality and accessible products
iii. Happy volunteer-members
iv. Equitable access to resources and wealth
v.   Economic well-being and quality of life or community development
vi. Importance of active women
vii. Empowerment
viii.Fund Infusion

1.2. Operational objectives

These are subordinate objectives and should always flexible to changes in the community and volunteer-members dynamics, needs and situations, environment and other resources. They include the following objectives:

i.   Quality Products or services
ii. Continuous Flow of production and services
iii. Empowerment, hatching of and innovation by teams and individual members;
iv. Balanced Human input in the factory
v.   Conducive Manufacturing space
vi. Accommodation Raw materials supplied by indigents
vii. Quantity of consumers' order and forecasted consumption for contingency and or stocks

viii. Lead time and distribution design, and

ix. Eliminate waste.

2. Principles of Planning

The principles of planning must have the following characteristics:

2.1. Relevant. Identification of major factors for analysis of the community. Needs. Source of Needs. Problems. Alternatives.

Necessary conditions for effective Entrepreneurship.

i. (For existing firms) A significant pressure or demand for change in an organisation's internal environment (e.g. labour unrest, CBA, unhappy/unsatisfied low-paid or insufficiently-paid employees; or tenants-landlord relationship (contracted or illegally detained properties; threatened tenures of labourers and tenants.)

    ii. Active involvement and collaboration in problem-identification (diagnosis) and solution-planning among different levels and sectors of the firm or organization.

The class struggle or conflict of Marx and violent strategies of worker-revolutionists are opposed by Schumpeter with his Entrepreneurship as "a *nearest approach possible for modern (or civilized) human beings.*"

    iii. (For new organisations) Needs of the communities are not met or served due to non-existence of producer-providers and suppliers.

    iv. Needs are available in the communities but inaccessible to most inhabitants that cause poverty, malnourishment, diseases, social unrest or chaos, or lost peace and order.

    v. Evidence of short-term and long-term results (at least 3 years projection and forecasting for short-term) of entrepreneurial undertakings.

    vi. Support or protection of government from neoliberal policies of government (government must abandon the one-ideology-for-one-nation policy and principle, and must work within the multiple frameworks appropriate for specific sectors, communities and territories).

2.2. Responsive & Flexible. SWOT and KASH Analyses. Emergence of other needs and conditions from undertakings, public policy, market structure, etc. Make a plan, organize, lead and control your plan and to change your plan cycle is flexibility and responsive to what is appropriate ahead of plans.

2.3. Realistic. Organisational and operational objectives and actions to be taken must be realistic, e.g., pluralist perspective (organizational) of socialism vs. worldwide socialism, basic quality products vs. high value added luxury products, etc.

2.4. Simple and Measurable. Products should avoid to be labelled as "commodity fetishism" and must be measurable for quality assurance.

115

2.5. Revolutionary and Visionary. Vision, mission and Goals must be clearly stated.

2.6. Time-bounded. Every task should have its progress and end. Schedules and deadlines are necessary for planning.

3. KASH Analysis

The Entrepreneur must conduct self-assessment prior to SWOT analysis to determine his or her Knowledge, Attitude, Skills and Habits in preparation and easy adjustments and improvements come SWOT factors are determined.

The same KASH assessment must be used in human resources recruitment for training needs analysis.

4. SWOT Analysis

The entrepreneur must start his or her plan by examining the different (existing or potential) factors inside and outside the organization (existing or for set-up). These factors are classified into Strengths, Weaknesses, Opportunities and Threats.

The factors to be examined inside the organisation are the Strengths and which can also be the Weaknesses. These are the following:

4.1. Strengths

1. Human Resources
2. Land
3. Commitment of Members
4. Knowledge and Skills
5. Technology
6. Management system
7. Fund, etc.

4.2. Weaknesses

1. Human Resources
2. Land
3. Commitment of Members
4. Knowledge and Skills
5. Technology
6. Management system
7. Fund, etc.

The factors to be examined outside the organisation are the Opportunities which can be Threats also. These are the following:

4.3. Opportunities

1. Miserable poor community
2. High unemployment rate
3. High poverty incidence
4. Government anti-poverty programs (relevant and responsive to local resources)
5. Private partnerships, etc.

4.4. Threats

1. Miserable poor community
2. High unemployment rate
3. High poverty incidence
4. Government anti-poverty programs (neoliberal ways)
5. Private partnerships, etc.

The Strengths can be Weaknesses if, let us say, Human Resources are not skilled or not fit for job physically and mentally due to harsh realities in life in which they marched throughout their lifetime. The ignorance of use of technology or resources can be weaknesses. The volunteers, employees, members and families are strength of the organization but can be the weakness at the same time. When these strengths can be weaknesses? While members and families are strengths for a large number of potential human resources is available, volunteers can be weakness if they are not yet trained and fit for the work. Volunteers' status as employees is weakness for anytime they will leave their duties and the necessary skills complementing others; will be left emptied. The Entrepreneur must translate this Weakness into Strength by providing adequate training, and recovery program.

The Opportunities can be Threats in a situation like Government anti-poverty program aimed to provide livelihood program implement within a neoliberal perspective like what International Fund for Agricultural Development (IFAD) do with its program that promote sari-sari or convenient stores for farmers selling MNC's products from coffee to soap instead of promoting collective farming to produce their basic needs for self-sufficiency.

The Threat of high unemployment rate or poverty is a threat to safety and order of the area but this must be translated by the Entrepreneur to Opportunity to provide employment and generate abundant supply of human resources.

The stakeholders inside and outside the organisations like supplier, customers, volunteers and members can be the organisation's SWOT. Government, an opportunity for funding and technical provision, can use her apparatus against the entrepreneurial organization to sabotage or stop or delay or prohibit from operating (Cooperative Development Authority is a neo-liberal agency in disguise of cooperative. We will discuss this as one of the barriers in the next Chapter.). A government administering the public in a neo-liberal framework, is totalitarian and tyrant which will not allow any progressive undertaking to pressure the poor and oppressed embrace the neo-liberal way of survival.

Media are also an opportunity for strategic ally for acceptance of and public information, and alternative advertising which are critical in reshaping the "common sense" of the proletariat and intellectuals. Media however can be a threat to the entrepreneurial organization if it is operated by capitalist-owners and stockholders who can push for policies to ban progressive products from advertising and launch black propaganda.

Academic institutions are also opportunities for inclusion of correct and authentic entrepreneurship in the curriculum but a threat in keeping the public particularly the students blind and astray.

Neighbouring communities are opportunities to have entrepreneurial organisations relevant to their communities. Their resources can complement the entrepreneurial organization requirements and can be another alternative source of supplies, another entrepreneurial suppliers by innovating their own production organisations. They can be threat as well if they are controlled by neo-liberal production and market. The supplies necessary for entrepreneurial production may not be accessible or available for progressive objectives. Weaknesses and threats can be converted to strengths and opportunities with correct attitudes and appropriate knowledge and skills.

Other suppliers of same products (or services) are usually threats to business entities but not threats to entrepreneurship. Some suppliers are not threats but can be strategic allies. The following is a story that will give you an idea how.

I had a conversation with my old-time friend who is a

121

public teacher. I informed her about this book. I told her that this is a different entrepreneurship. This book may be available in amazon, kindle, Barnes and noble, etc.

Our conversation is our example. My book is distributed though hi-tech and for the rich market, I informed her. A buyer or getter must have money, debit or credit card to purchase a copy of my book online. My book is accessible at a price. This price includes the cost of book production and the commission fees and profit margin of the retailers and distributors.

What is this book all about? A part, I told her, "...my book encourages "market innovation" Poor people will benefit a lot from innovation." The basic needs like food or rice or meat are getting inaccessible to poor people due to rising prices caused by the costs in the middle---distributors and retailers' costs, mark-up or profit margin.

It is obvious that my book is professing entrepreneurship and management principles for abolition of middle market costs to make products and services less expensive and accessible to all. At this point of time, generational, and generally, all markets are for rich people. There is no place or channel that bring goods to poor consumers at a price proportion to their meagre income. All prices are determined by the supply and demand, or by the sellers' discretion. No commodities are priced determined by the poor buyers based on their purchasing powers. Poor are deprived of their needs and of my book (most probably) but not really nor completely deprived.

If middle costs are not favourable for the poor, why am I using the service of the e-stores like lulu, amazon, etc.?

I am approving Walzer's idea of not abolishing the market or system if the people suffered from market tyranny. We should not fight tyranny with tyranny neither evil with evil.

Separation and fences are necessary for justice to bring harmony as Michael Walzer emphasised it in his work.

This book of mine, as well as my other books (like any other commodities, e.g. rice, meat, etc.) should remain in a distribution system operated by and within the market for the rich (expensive, unaffordable prices, debit or credit card accessibility). To keep the status quo is justice for the rich. But what about the poor? An innovated market or middle-cost-free distribution system will be established for the poor where goods (rice, meat, etc.,) including my book and services will be available, accessible to poor people at a very

123

affordable price. Although the prices are most likely to be less by 20-50%, the rice and meat will remain at the same function, quality and same measurement so as my book. Product innovation is required to ensure the same quality in which equality and justice among rich and the poor is guaranteed.

The price discrimination, process, methods, places or territories for distribution and purchases; protocols of terms of payments (cards, checks, e-payments, etc. for wealthy people can be used to finely defined the lines from cash in small amount or labour skills, calculation in natura of the less privileged consumers) are good separations and fences to bring justice to both and all people. No one must be deprived of life support. Everyone must enjoy economic well-being and have improvements in the quality of life.

Reverse discrimination is to be part of market innovation. Memberships of poor people must be required to determine the eligibility of enjoying the benefits offered by innovated market of entrepreneurship.

If the poor are discriminated in debit and credit cards purchase system and high prices of some stores the rich people are discriminated in membership cards purchase system and low price of entrepreneurial stores.

3.2. Organising Function

An entrepreneur or group of entrepreneurs, after careful planning will start with human resources analysis for organizing. People in the communities are equipped with varied knowledge and skills and personalities and characters to be of help in carrying the change or economic development in the communities. Making head counting and inventory of human resources---strength and weakness, tangible and intangible, to know who can do what tasks, how weakness can be translated to strength (e.g. aged, old and differently-abled persons). KY (Know yourself... know your resources...) Analysis as in KASH is of great importance in organising.

1. Human Resources Analysis

In business management, there are qualifications and minimum requirements for a person to be able part of the organisation's work force or human resources. On the contrary, entrepreneurial management is not selective and particular with exact or fit-for-job persons. Entrepreneurs look at the people, all adult people in the community as potential human resources of organization to be changed

125

(OD from capitalist to entrepreneurial) or newly established. This includes the women and men, aged, retirees or fresh graduates, migrants or indigenous, schooled or unschooled, skilled or unskilled, experienced or inexperienced, professional or novice, employed or unemployed, physically wholly abled or differently-abled persons. Entrepreneurs are able to employ anyone and make use of their available resources (knowledge, skills, expertise, etc.) and potentials for the organization. Costs or risks are not the concerns of Entrepreneurs. Monopoly is the purpose of entrepreneurship and not competition. BOS is for Entrepreneurs' consideration to create new "markets."

2. People and Organisation

Dealing with people with different aspirations, interests, background, experiences, orientations and perceptions is the most difficult task ever in my life. Socialisation from early age, formal education, knowledge and professional experience are not enough to understand the people and the way they behave in diverse situations. Different backgrounds include religious, political, cultural and moral preferences and beliefs. Backgrounds shaped our values and attitudes and constructed our culture. This culture affects our behaviour. This behaviour strongly affects our choice of goods and services to consume and work or employment to do. A person's desire for a particular product can be driven by the cultural acceptance and influence, while inclination to particular work or employment is due to pay, prestige or cultural acceptance and influence as well.

Cultures shape environment and environment shapes cultures. Culture and environment determine our behaviour. These are true but not all the time or not to all people. Some people behave as a response to intrinsic stimuli ---values or motivations. This intrinsic stimuli include values and beliefs which sometimes control ones behaviour to respond to perceived information. Some behaves differently.

Business managers are not burdened with these multi-preferences and diversified cultures of people. They just formulate policies to serve the set goals and objective of the organization and reject or fire whoever in contradiction of them, disregard the culture, religion and morals.

Entrepreneurs are facing a great challenge in life if not a burden nor a cross and Calvary. It is less difficult in rural or countryside areas than urban or metropolitan areas where business environment dominates the economic activities.

Organisations in urban areas are more formal and structured than any other organization in rural areas. However, organisations, either situated in urban or rural areas are consist of people or groups of people working together for specific purposes to achieve organisational objectives in the organizations and for individual personal objectives.

Organisations are guided by its own set of rules usually framed in vision and mission, philosophy and culture statements to be carried by responsible persons who are usually the chairman or CEO in business organisations, executives and managers, while vision and mission of organisations in innovation or entrepreneurship .are to be carried by all members. Organisations' behaviours usually are reflections of set vision and missions, philosophy and culture and members' shared values and beliefs and behaviours.

Organisations'' success relies in people because it is the people who plan, decide, implement for the interest, survival, and success of the organisations.

3. Types of Organisation

Type of organization is critical in organizing. The organizational dynamic and freedom is limited to what is allowed by the governing laws appropriate for the organization. There are Private, Public and Not-for-Profit organisations. They are classified into Limited Company or Sole Proprietorship, Corporation, Partnership or Cooperative. Limited Company or Sole Proprietorship and Cooperative are most appropriate for Entrepreneurial organization. There are not-for-profit organizations under the non-stock and non-profit corporations or associations.

4. Organisational Culture

"[T]he link between the organization of work and the organization of culture was rather envisaged by Gramsci as the new 'professional culture', the new technical and vocational preparation needed by manpower (from the skilled worker to the manager) to control and to lead industrial development, as well as the society which this development inevitably generates."

-Monasta (2000)-

129

Cultures shape environment and environment shapes cultures. Culture and environment determine our behaviours. Behaviours constructed a culture.

How can we create a cultural hegemony or professional culture from a traditional or prevailing culture of the organization or community? What is the acceptable or ideal culture? To understand this with real-life examples, let us first familiarize the different dimensions of culture.

The Six (6) Dimensions of Culture identified by Rowe (2008):

1. Stories
2. Symbols
3. Routines
4. Power Structures
5. Organisational Structures
6. Control systems

Stories reveal the organisation's best and worst scenarios and protagonists and villains. Tyrant managers and executives or office Dilbert behaviours are classified as bad by those who recognize what is good. Stories creates attitudes among people who to believe and who are not.

The symbols are the logo, seal of the organization, and the furniture, offices, gardens, lobby, hallway, appliances, etc. These help create cultural change.

Routines are the usual daily activities of members and volunteers. Anyone who come for work, works and that work represents responsibility and responsible culture to meet everyone's expectations.

Structures develop culture the way power and organizational structures are used. The power are usually associated to those who are in much more responsibility in the organizational structure. They are the supervisors, managers and executives. These people having the power can create a culture of professionals among the labourer level or production line. That is why entrepreneur is encouraged not to detach from the workers.

Control system (Evaluation) as a dimension of culture, can develop habits (negative or positive) that construct the culture. Progressive Evaluation can eliminate negative habits and develop positive habits and relationships among workers and different departments.

Positive attitudes of members build the organizational culture. The positive attitudes of the members must be reconfirmed, reshaped, and performed. The following but not limited to such are some attitudes that must be visible from and can be performed by members without reservations:

1. Altruistic
2. Helpful
3. Faithful
4. Honest
5. Empathic
6. Loyal
7. Trustful
8. Integrity
9. Ethical
10. Moral
11. Compassion, and
12. Respectful.

Respect for every member of the organization is a recognition of organization as a system. Any poor performance of any member can affect the performance of the whole. Any negative behaviour can affect others behaviour negatively.

Some organisations clearly declared or expressed organizational culture in an organizational statement along with Vision and Mission statements like:

"We firmly believe in our commitment, collective leadership and respect for each other are the foundations of our success."

"We value the essence and integrity of our human resources on top of any other resources of our organization."

5. Organisational Structure

Organisational structure for Entrepreneurial Organisation is different from Business Organisations. Business organizational structures depend on types of organization registered to regulatory body. The Business corporation and partnership affairs are decided by the majority interests of the stockholders or partners. This decision making powers are delegated to the fiduciary agents ---chairpersons, presidents, members of the board of directors and to the organisations' fiduciary agents in the persons of managers and executives. These type of organization practice democracy but based on number or amount of ownership.

Majority ownership or stock prevail over the minority. The social contract of owners with managers (chairman, president or managing director, etc.) give the managers the power to make decisions and prioritise agenda deemed necessary for the attainment of set goals and objectives. These fiduciary agents in return, are responsible and accountable to the owners and stockholders. Faithfulness and loyalty the owners and stockholders are guaranteed and must be and always above any others' interests may it be in contradiction to own beliefs, ethics and morals.

The objective for profit generation as perceived as a right of every investor, accepted as primary duty of the fiduciary agents, subordinates the objective of paying the employees with decent salaries and wages.

Structured organizations like these are effective in strategic operations and competitions.

Limited company or sole proprietorship organization is singlehandedly decided by the owner. Employees' interests are always subordinated to the owner's. The structure is simple and like the corporations varies dependent on size and tasks involve in operations. Owner can have his her own manager and can chose to stay at the back of the stage show or can be on top of the organization. This type of organization can breed more entrepreneurs from the ranks of owners and employees alike experience multi-tasking works and responsibilities.

The cooperative is most likely appropriate for it is regulated in a different manner and with different laws outside the capitalist laws. The disadvantage however of this type is the vulnerability of the organization to abuse of shares ownerships which guarantees pro-rated shares from surplus by members who are more capable of acquiring shares than other members. And any member can be a member even without direct participation or direct human resources contribution. This capitalist features of cooperative threatens the equitable distributions surplus of members. This capitalist features of cooperatives can be remedied in the Articles of Cooperation and By-Laws particularly the provisions on memberships, duties and benefits, and the shares ownership can be limited to what is equitable. Policy on honoraria or compensations for volunteers or members can be set based on each one's family needs.

The decision making process in cooperative is just like the corporation but based on the number of members instead of stocks. The cooperative manager is the fiduciary agent of the cooperative who is entrusted and delegated with power to decide and set priorities for the attainment of set goals and objectives consistent to superordinate objectives of the organisation. Some cooperatives are for profit. Thus the cooperative manager has the duty the same with that of corporate CEO's.

The entrepreneurial organization in cooperative form, the cooperative manager or the entrepreneur can aim for profitless operations. He or she can set objectives at break-even with employees' just salaries and wages expenses, volunteers' compensations, indigenous' supplies just costs, and accessible price for the members and community inhabitants. This arrangement can be used also in limited company or sole proprietorship.

.   The entrepreneur must use dictatorial or authoritarian approach but with humane and empowering strategies and sensitive to others ideas. Democratic approach or decision of the majority is not always accurate (most of the time, inappropriate and unjust) and difficult to be evaluated and lack of accountability. Critical organizational decisions should be made by the entrepreneur-manager and should not require members' majority vote. The departments and teams critical to their responsibilities shall be decided by themselves.

This entrepreneur will disappear from the scene come the organization's self-reliance with members empowered, collectively lead each other, managing self, realised and live as part of the whole organization, well-being and enjoying the quality of life.. The entrepreneur can leave and look for another entrepreneurial activity in other communities or can stay and live as part of the whole organization and community, no longer an undertaker because the function of the Entrepreneur ends when change is completed.

The different structures presented can be summarized in centralised and decentralised organisations.

The entrepreneurial organization can best work in decentralized authority in line with collective leadership. The entrepreneur-manager therefore must be able to identify which departments or teams (in business, there are temporary and permanent teams) to be organized and be given the line and staff authority.

Line authority for line departments are essentials for vital departments like production department, sales or distribution department, and or finance are critical to survival and growth of the organisation and they are empowered and can function autonomously.

137

These line departments may or may not be supported by staff departments which staff authority is to help the line departments' activities. For example, the production department, a line department and authority may need or need not the assistance of supply or purchasing department, a staff department. Maintenance of supply department is costly and fit competitive market of suppliers from community, local, national to offshores. Innovation of source of supplies (practically excluding OEM's) as discussed in the challenges facing the entrepreneur, will eliminate the market costs and may organize the community to produce materials for production utilizing idle resources such as land and human resources.

Sales (and or distribution where members and volunteers are paid partly with goods, or the so called calculations in natura or kind) department, another line department with line authority can operate on its own dynamic will not need the support and assistance of marketing department (a staff department and authority) based on a newly structured market changed by the entrepreneur-manager.

6. Operational Structures

With the description of the departments and authorities, let us illustrate them into operational structures (discussed earlier is organisational structure). The entrepreneurial Organisation may use one (1) or two (2) or more structure at the same time dependent on the present practical situation of the organization.

One structure suitable for entrepreneurial operation is **Function Structure:**

Figure 1. Function Structure

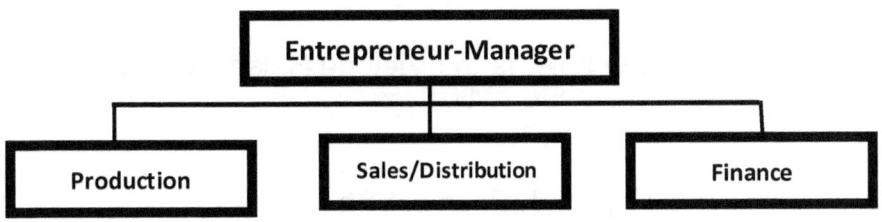

This requires division of labour and specialization for each department. Duties and responsibilities for each department are clearly defined and volunteers are focused on their own areas. Each department is responsible for their functions and directly report to the entrepreneur-manager for any concerns in each department.

Functional Structure can be combined with another operational structure to define the role of each production line, or this **Product Structure** can be used instead of Functional Structure and let us take the Farm organization as an example:

Figure 2. Product Structure A

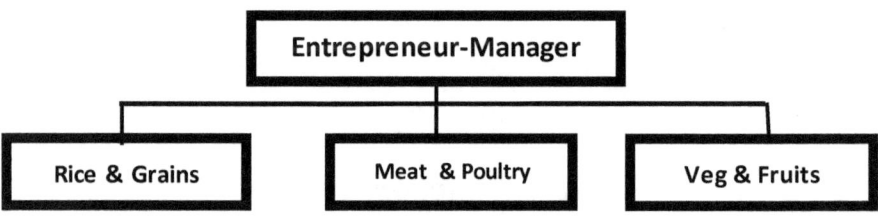

Or for another example, is the Victoria Helena's Amazons:

Figure 3. Product Structure B

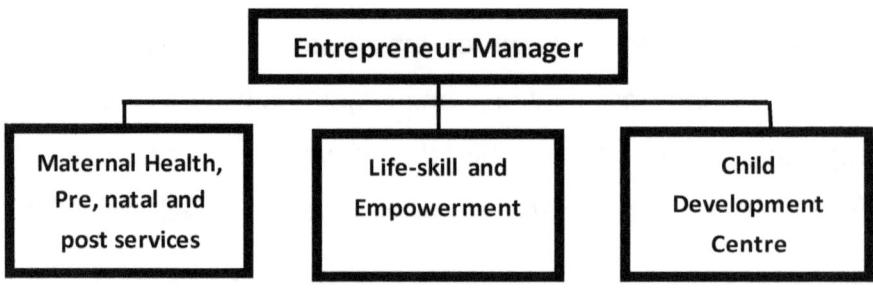

The **Product Structure** requires volunteers to do multi-tasking duties from production, to distribution to financial and accounting. Volunteers in each product can set their own objectives (e.g. quantity, variety to be produced) based on their resources and forecasted demand. The production areas for each product can be set-up in different locations. Each shall report to the Entrepreneur-Manager.

Another operational structure useful for entrepreneurial organization is the **Geographical Structure**. This can be used together with Functional or Product structures or to both:

Figure 4. Geographical Structure A

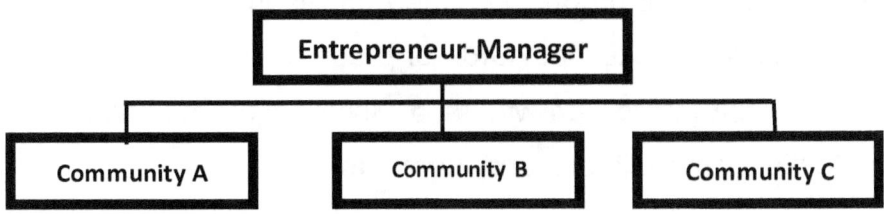

Or for another geographical strategy:

Figure 5. Geographical Structure B

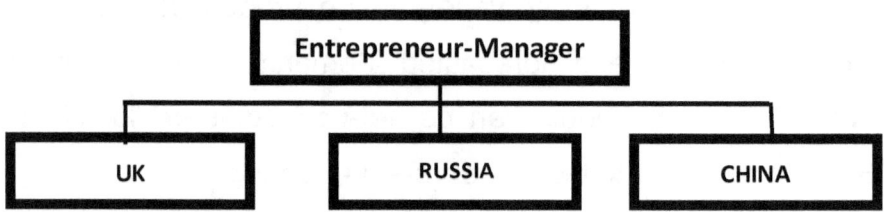

The **Geographical Structure** can make sub-structures for their territorial operations. This type of structure is beneficiary-focused type. It address the cultural diversity and specific needs. Its tendency to customized products and or services will help prevent or save each territory from alienation. Each territorial operation, volunteers can make their own way of producing based on resources at hand and at reach and make standards of procedures and still flexible and sensitive to growth and innovative methods and potentials of volunteers and members.

Of course, each operational structure and combination has its own disadvantages. The entrepreneur-manager has to decide which is which based on practicality and logical approach towards the attainment of set goals and objectives. Flexibility of plans and adaptability to change and growth can help things easier and realistic to reach. Self-alienation and failure of organisations mostly due to closed and one-correct-line of thinking or 'infallible' attitudes of managers.

7. Teams

To lighten the weight of the entrepreneurs' herculean tasks, Teams are necessary for the plans to be implemented. Entrepreneurs are expected to be knowledgeable in organising teams. Teams must be have at least the following characteristics:

1. With specific set objectives;
2. Effective communication system;
3. With logical plan;
4. Team motivations;
5. Empowered to make decisions and set priorities;
6. Teamwork, delegation and assistance to teammates.
7. Team vision consistent to Organisational vision;
8. Leadership
9. Management
10. Care and patience for each team member

143

11. Push-up or pull-up others for success

12. Have fun

I learned from my experiences during the times when most of my journeys with people got lost. There must be something wrong why I see nobody beside, behind nor in front of me for they are left along the way of our travel, scattered, adventured and conform to where they are now.

The quality circles of Japanese management must be taken into consideration by entrepreneur-manager to benefit each member for attitude reformation and organizational culture adaptation. Members must have trainings and equipped with necessary knowledge and skills prior to deployment on board to ensure effectiveness and defence against deviations or destructions. According to Knowles (2011) the Japanese circles is expressed as "It is better for a hundred people to take one step than for one person to take a hundred steps."

An entrepreneur is not an entrepreneur if he or she doesn't walk with the workers which businessmen do.

An organic intellectual must have a unique sense instead of common sense to remain with the planks of the workers and communities. Workers and members tend to scatter, adventured and conform to outside norms and traditions, start of weakening foundations of the teams and organization as a whole.

8. Hiring, Training, Evaluation, Retaining or Transfer

The business-manager *is "responsible for the application and performance of knowledge"*

-Peter F. Drucker-

That is why business organisations hire people in accordance to its standard of qualification, knowledge and skills.

The way Drucker defines a manager, business managers will never hire illiterates, unschooled, unskilled, neither the disable (differently-able) people. Knowledge for application and performance must be useful to business. Business trainings are given to people with minimum qualifications for assimilations to the organization but never to people who will cost much more than the training budget of the organization.

The entrepreneurial-manager hires anyone in the

community who is willing to work as volunteer. Any applicant who does not fit for the job or job requirements will be his or her responsibility. Illiteracy, let us say, which is one common problem why a big number of people are idle and are not working, is confronted by the entrepreneur-manager. Adult and aged people in the countryside are shy or reluctant to work in any formal organisation because of this shortcomings. An entrepreneur-manager develops training program inside the organization for the hired illiterate people but is not satisfied with it and further launch literacy program in the community for families of the illiterate volunteers. Providing the organization with scarce expertise and labour hours and providing the human resources with the healthy and happy experiences.

Business managers hire people as employees on regular & contractual, permanent or temporary basis while entrepreneurial managers hire people as volunteers on permanent basis. Entrepreneurial managers can hire employees' expertise which are not immediately available in the community on a contractual or temporary basis. It is the organisation's strategy to attract employees to stay permanently as volunteers and lifetime member of the organization.

Training is always important for empowerment and collective undertakings. Members will be equipped through training to complement other members for the attainment of objectives, making each one supportive and kind to one another. Training is not just for knowledge and skills acquisition but also for values and cultural formation.

Criticism-self-criticism and open forums can also help individuals to move forward for the teams to move forward for organisation to move forward.

Assessment however is not intended for termination or dismissal like what business managers do. Entrepreneurs use it for control, development and finding and hatching potentials or aptitudes of members, and finding the right place or position for each member success and find what each one might be good at in any given position or opportunity to try something new.

9. Facilities, Technology and Equipment

Facilities, technology and equipment are made for human productivity, safety and convenience. They are made to serve human beings never to antagonize, threat neither displace nor make unproductive. Existing organisations for

Entrepreneurship have existing facilities, technology and equipment, All must be reassessed for the existing workers possible adjustments to the changes to happen and for community's needs and provide any necessary changes to fit for the required products and methods of productions, and job inflows. My earlier comments to McDonald's can be a good case sample in addition to the impact of innovated methods to productivity that will shorten the working hours of the workers for them to have more quality times to their self (inclusive the leisure time), families and community.

The entrepreneurial organisation that will start from the scratch in a community is quite difficult. The entrepreneur-manager shall identify and plan for creation or acquisition of necessary facilities, technology and equipment to produce the identified needed products by the community in consideration to the available human resources whether fit or unfit but trainable and capable.

10. Materials

Materials are usually supplied by contractors---local or offshore, outside the community of the organisation's location. Upon launching Entrepreneurship, these contractors of supplies discontinue supplying. The entrepreneur-manager has to identify the necessary materials and source from indigenous producer-suppliers in the community. If the supply is not present in the community, re-create or organize another group of indigenous community inhabitants to produce necessary materials for production inputs applicable. Thus, the Entrepreneur–manager is not detached from the community but a part of the mass transforming or providing knowledge, skills, eliciting positive attitudes, and giving clear vision and paths to their well-being and quality life.

Entrepreneurship is in disconformity against Adam's Smith's "buying is better than producing" principle which keep the resources idling and make the people dependent to products and services offered by neoliberal organisations. The Entrepreneur-manager makes idle resources productive for the community inhabitants' benefits.

11. Quality Management

Product innovation is quality management. Entrepreneurship's product innovation is geared towards accessibility of the product in terms of price by the poor community and volunteers through cost efficiency and productivity. This is discussed also in my comment to McDonald's and can be taken for case sample development.

The capitalist-oriented market or neoliberal competition pressures the business organisations like McDonald's to create attractive, different products in terms of specifications, functions, added value and features and adopt fashionable packaging for the *qualified market*'s attention and patronage. Entrepreneurship, on the contrary, will eliminate unnecessary costs without sacrificing the basic functions and standards of the product with adherence and commitment to continuous improvement. Entrepreneurship aimed for equal access of the products by the community inhabitants and this is to include the market innovation by eliminating the middle market costs from supply of input materials to finished products. In communities for start-up organisations, consider the concept of Blue Ocean Strategy that "*denotes all industries not in existence---unknown market space, untainted by competitions*" developed by W. Chan Kim and Renee Mauborgne (2004).

3.3. Leading Functions

Any business organisation requires a strong leader with good managerial skills. On the other hand, Entrepreneurial organizations require all members to be a leader and be equipped with managerial knowledge and skills for self-management and collective leadership. I don't see any traditional leadership style that will fit for Entrepreneurial organization. Collective leadership which is different from others is the most effective leadership style for Entrepreneurial organization. Some leadership styles however are useful and appropriate for application of Entrepreneur in certain situations. These include "transformational", "participatory" and "autocratic" leadership styles.

Management vs. Leadership

Let us make a sharp distinction between management and leadership to avoid confusion along the way of entrepreneurial journey.

Management is the ability or skill to plan, organize, lead and control and attain the set goals and objectives while leadership is the ability or skill to envision and ability to bring the organization to that vision.

Organisational vision of entrepreneurial organisation is a shared vision of every member. Every member is walking at one's own pace but all in the same direction with the resources, knowledge, skills and ingenuity available at hand, managing self for the attainment of set goals and objectives. This kind of ability to bring oneself with other members, and the whole organisation towards a set vision and objectives is **leadership.**

While management is basically a verb or action of a person who is a manager, leadership is basically an adjective or quality or character of leading by a person who is a leader. Management and leadership sometimes are used as noun if referred to authority and power. One must be a good leader to be a good manager. One must not be a good manager to be a good leader. Thus, a worker---technical, clerical or by any nature of task can be a good leader without being a manager, and no one can be a manager if he or she can't be a good leader.

A leader corrects the wrong things done while manager does the right things for the things to be done. A leader does not know or uncertain about the things ahead but courageous to take pace forward. A good manager anticipates negative things ahead to happen and tries to prevent them from happening.

What is Collective Leadership?

"I start with the premise that the function of leadership is to produce more   leaders and not more followers."

-Ralph Nader-

The Collective Leadership

I have discussed in our leading topic introduction that every member is walking at one's own pace (without being directed) but all in the same direction with the resources, knowledge, skills and ingenuity available at hand, managing self for the attainment of set goals and objectives. This kind of ability to bring oneself with other members, and the whole organisation towards a set vision and objectives is **leadership.** *This is Collective Leadership---* **leadership by all members.**

An entrepreneur must have multiple characters and multiple leadership styles to achieve this kind of leadership which is collective. He or she must be persuasive enough through demonstration of particular knowledge or skill in any given time or situation to organisation members or volunteer-workers and let them realize the things and aspects behind of what they are doing and what they are not doing. The starting point for the entrepreneur is to conduct trainings for members and volunteer-workers to have the basic knowledge about collective leadership. It must be understood by everyone that it is everyone's responsibility to carry oneself towards set goals and objectives. Everyone must understand the organization as a system, and anyone who failed to avoid oneself to be a baggage or burden to any member or volunteer will mean system or organization failure. It is everyone's responsibility to do what is due and required to do without being directed. Individual freedom and autonomy are enjoyed but they entail responsibilities to common good of the organization.

Information is the basic requirement for collective leadership and these information must be analysed and translated to objectives and for understanding of everyone in the organization. This may start from how many units of products to be produced per day to supply the need of members and families of volunteer-workers? How are these to be obtained? How much input are necessary? How much are available? How much in-process materials I will prepare for use by the persons or stations next to my work station? How will I avoid wastes? and so on. Every work does not require close supervision.

In going to this status, the entrepreneur may apply other leadership styles. These may be the Transformational, Autocratic, and Participatory Leadership Style. Each one has its own advantages and disadvantages in any particular organisational structure and situation:

Transformational Leadership

Transformational leadership, according to Copeland (2014) is the first and most noteworthy leadership style that explicitly incorporated an ethical and moral component in leader behaviour. Burns(1978) theorized that a leader in such style, *"appeal to and influence the moral values of the [members] and inspire them to reform and revamp their organizations...,*creates and sustains a context that maximizes human and organizational capabilities; facilitate multiple levels of transformation (innovation); and align them with core values and a unified purpose."

Avolio, Waldman and Yammarino (1991) Lowe, Kroeck, & Sivasubramaniam, (1996) established the transformational leadership as a concept of inspirational motivation, and intellectual stimulation, and studied and examined a large number of research studies and concluded that transformational leadership enhances subordinate motivation and performance.

While Bass & Steidlmeier (1999) emphasized that to be truly transformational, a leader must also be moral, ethical and authentic, Carless, Wearing & Mann (2000) described a transformational leader as one that: (a) communicates a vision, (b) develops staff, (c) provides support, (d) empowers staff, (e) is innovative, (f) leads by example, and (g) is charismatic.

Autocratic Leadership Style

This style does not mean curtailing one's freedom. An entrepreneur-manager retains as much power and decision-making authority as possible as an organic intellectual in-the process of creating a professional culture. Trainings are mostly done autocratically but this should not impair everyone's self-discovery and self-realisation and hatching and innovative ability enhancement.

Sometimes members and volunteers are encouraged to obey instructions without receiving any explanations to encourage self-discovery and realization.

Autocratic does not always mean punitive. Any offense or failure of any member or volunteer must be dealt with criticism-self-criticism and trainings.

Participative Leadership Style

Entrepreneurial participative leadership is different from traditional participative leadership which members participates in decision making which is more identified as democratic leadership. In contrast to traditional participative leadership, which believed that participatory decision-making improves the understanding of the issues involved by those who must carry out the decisions, the entrepreneurial participative is still autocratic leadership in decision-making. The participative aspect is on the entrepreneurs' participation in labour tasks, community life, production, and distribution, and so on, for the entrepreneur's understanding and realization of things within and around those mentioned. His or her participation will give a more meaningful comprehensions in entrepreneurial and managerial perspectives to create new process, procedures, and strategies for decision-making. The traditional participative which is democratic is not effective for the individual members' perceptions differ from one another and decide on different perspectives most of the time, subjective.

3.4. Evaluation Function

I use Evaluation as another function of Management instead of Control function.

Weinbach (1994) argued that Control is sometimes seen as an infringement of autonomy of the individual worker and is basically designed to do that. It is universally resented, especially by mature professionals whose functions are to guard their autonomy and their right to exercise professional discretion.

Control, as a function of management, I can say, is not about directing or manipulating the action of the people in the organization by the person responsible like manager or supervisor. Not even what other people think as curtailing one's freedom or empowering. For Mullins (2005), *"control is a process that involves a systematic process through which managers can compare real performance with plans, standards and objectives and take corrective action if deviations occur."*

and it is the most appropriate definitions among several different definitions of control in management literature.

Anthony (1965) explains that *"Management control is the process by which managers assure that resources are obtained and used effectively and efficiently in the accomplishment of the organization's objectives and it involves "getting things done."*

According to Hoefstede (1968), several management authors kept the original French meaning for control which is *inspection*. Inspection is a process of assessment or evaluation. Let us use the term Evaluation in a fashionable manner to avoid the negative connotation of Control.

1. Two Levels of Evaluation

There are two (2) levels of evaluation. These are the following:

1.1. Organisational Evaluation. It concerns with the organisation's total effectiveness and efficiency in progress and extent of attaining the superordinate objectives and goals (vision, mission, culture etc.), and

1.2. Operational Evaluation. It concerns with the organisation's activities that involves production of goods and or services to the consumers.

2. Evaluation Process

Evaluation Process is basically consist of four (4) stages, namely;

    2.1. Setting Standards;

    2.2. Evaluation & Auditing;

    2.3. Recording;

    2.4. Corrective Action, CSC, Learning, Realignment; or Change of Plan, or upon perfect execution or on track in progress or in-process or meeting the standards and objectives; the next stage after Auditing and Recording is:

    2.5. Reinforcement, Motivation and or Celebration.

This process may vary or change, may be more than 4 stages depending on the objectives and operational activities, and standards of the organization. Each stage may involve multiple stages and evaluation activities.

The figure 6 illustrates the evaluation process.

Figure 6.Evaluation Process

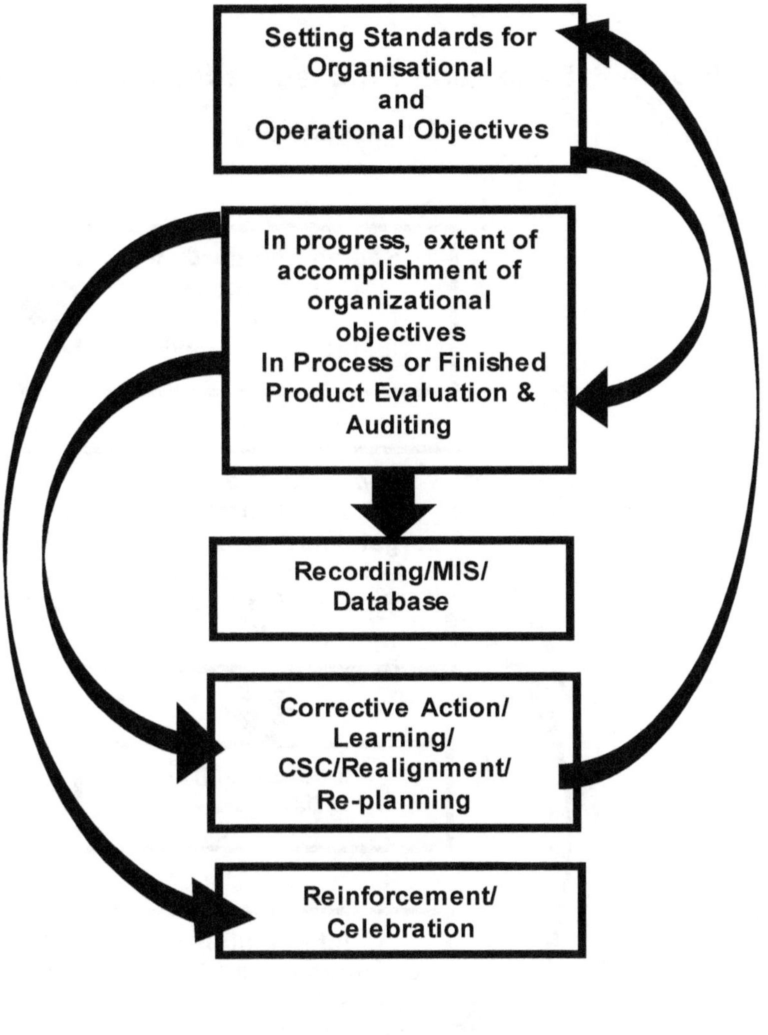

Setting Standards for Organisational and Operational Objectives

In progress, extent of accomplishment of organizational objectives In Process or Finished Product Evaluation & Auditing

Recording/MIS/ Database

Corrective Action/ Learning/ CSC/Realignment/ Re-planning

Reinforcement/ Celebration

Let us take Victoria Helena's Amazon for Another example .

Figure 7. Evaluation Process for Service-oriented Organisation

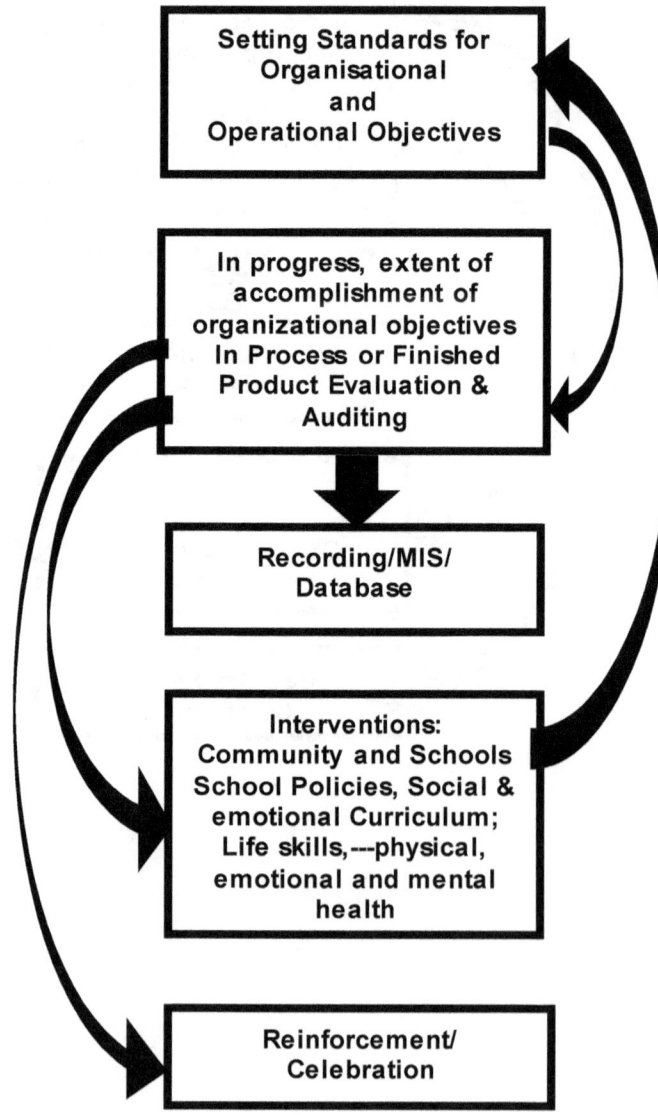

2.1. Setting Standards

The first step of Evaluation is to determine standards in which the measured behaviour, process, material and product specifications, quality, quantity, service progress, etc., will be compared. Let us get some objectives we have set in Planning stage.

2.1.1. Happy volunteer-members and

2.1.2. Economic well-being and quality of life or community development

These two examples of organisational objectives expressed in general terms must be specified in measurable and realistic statements or standards, these can be translated into Operational objectives like the following examples:

1. Sufficient Income for families of volunteer-members aimed to at least PhP750.00/day for a family of 4 and PhP500.00 for family of 2; work-life balance 6 hours a day or 36 hours a week, vacation and sick leave, monthly recreational activities, respect for everyone, clean, well-lighted and ventilated work stations, and

so on (of course all must be based on researched evidence particularly on the amount of income which is sufficient for a family of what size);

2. All children must be enrolled in school, elementary to college, all members, family must be healthy with monthly medical check-up, environmental, community health, sanitation and personal hygiene programs, decent shelter with individual bed and each household comfort room, access to clean drinking water, access to electricity, and so on.

Let us break the Operational objectives into three (3) specific Standards:

1. Quality Products. This can be the specific measurements in weight, size, colour, texture, and the most important feature is the function of the product. For example, meat, poultry or beef. Standards can be in 1 kilogram, must be reddish, frozen and fresh (production and expiration dates must be tagged to the products), and so on.

2. Quantity of consumers' order and forecasted consumption for contingency and or stocks. The quantity must be based on the need of the

organization (cost, break-even, etc.) volunteers, members and family and the communities. These must be expressed in numbers .e.g. 1 million kgs of beef, 1 million kgs of dressed chicken, per year and should be broken down to daily production monthly and quarterly;

3. Eliminate waste. This must be translated into procedural policy, in handling to avoid wasted materials, errors in specifications like under or overweight, etc., and quantitative analysis to avoid over production which turned out to be waste as they expired; and process standards like the step by step procedure, in-process standard handling, to avoid contamination and food poisoning.

These products are not limited to product specifications standards. The process standards which aimed for elimination of waste also aimed for eco-efficiency standards particularly the production of livestock, feeds and manure. Kondoh, Mishima, et. al. (2008) propose an index to evaluate real performance of products, by considering product's utility value, cost and environmental impact, throughout the product lifecycle. Efficiency indicator is named total performance indicator (TPI) for Total

Performance Analysis (TPA). This is involves additional stages and paper works for product and overall evaluation process.

2.2. Evaluation & Auditing

Measures matter most in evaluating performance output versus objectives. According to Quin (2014), in giving much importance on measurement, if some factor(s) are important for the organization, then there must be a way of measuring them. Performance Measurement system.

In Victoria Helena's Amazon's, the output or in-progress service can be measured also, like the meat producer, in qualitatively and quantitatively measurement through interview and examination, and reduced number of substance abusers, children and youth at sexual-risk, increase of enrolled children to schools, healthy behaviour and social relationship of mothers, and nutrition of both mother and infant child.

Both manufacturing and service entrepreneurial providers use statistics quantity and qualitative expert judgments based on set standards.

Evaluation involves several activities in different aspects of organizational and operational tasks. These include the following:

1. Performance Evaluation
2. Procedural Evaluation
3. Equipment & Technology Evaluation
4. Material Evaluation
5. Financial Evaluation

Organisational progress maybe best evaluated with the use of **Results Impact Management System (RIMS)** to measure the volunteer-workers, members and families' Household Assets Index, Malnutrition, literacy, etc.

2.3. Recording

Anything that is measured and evaluated must be recorded.

Using Management Information System (**MIS)** is very important for any organization, from human resources management to keep track of and evaluate costs and identify deviances, to distribution, and so on. Information was mentioned earlier as one of the basic essentials of collective leadership. MIS can be computerized or manual.

2.4. Corrective Action

Deviances of output, in progress results, and performances noticed, identified and audited as a result of evaluation are taken for analysis for necessary action to be taken. One of the several actions to be taken is corrective action.

2.4.1. Criticism-Self-Criticism.

This is a performance evaluation process popularized in communist and socialist organisations---a process of evaluating others' performances in a team or department or in an organization as a whole inclusive the performances of the entrepreneur-manager. The person evaluating is anyone who believes in his or her evaluation (or criticism) of others can help improve the organization, operations or particular production process in a **behavioural manner.** Criticising personal conduct of fellows should not be part of this evaluation process. After delivering (and recording) the performance evaluation, he or she must evaluate him/herself also in behavioural manner and proposed alternatives (change of plan or additional), or point to realignment and or corrective actions.

2.4.2. Learning. Realignment, Plan, Update Adjustments, or Change of Plan.

The process of evaluating and auditing the actual performances, output and progress, financial, costs etc. versus ideals---standards, objectives, etc., those who are involve must meditate, recall and analyse the things done, and realize and learn the why's, how's and what's and so on of the tasks done for the prevention from happening or committing the same errors or deviances, which can be translated to training programs and or policies, and or adjustments of plan for corrections (or for the same routines to be taken in the future in case of better or perfect performances and output). One cannot be blamed for miscalculation of production objective if the failure can be traced to materials or equipment. Some adjustments are required.

Corrective feedback must be given immediately without delay, as quick as in giving positive feedback or at the very moment the errors are noticed.

2.5. Reinforcement. Motivation. Celebration.

Positive feedback which includes sincere way of saying "thank you," "good work," is an intangible recognition and reward.

Recognition, rewards and celebration traditionally are used in leadership function of management. Let us use them in Evaluation Function instead. Celebrate each other, the achievements and the things done. Every task should have its own ending or closure. Members should know when the tasks ended. Members' performances can be controlled by motivations and reinforcements.

Ownership of the success and the whole organization will follow.

Chapter 4 Common Pitfalls and Barriers of Entrepreneurship

Every social stratum has its own 'common sense' and its own 'good sense'. Common sense is not something rigid and immobile, but is continually transforming itself, enriching itself with scientific ideas (empirical works and thoughts) and with philosophical opinions which have entered ordinary life. These philosophical syntheses however are most favoured and accepted by intellectuals and mass if it brings material benefits and comfort in their ordinary life. The neoliberalism as a philosophical synthesis dominated societies and established new conventions and culture which develops individual trait such as Allport's cardinal trait like greed, love of money, power hungry, individualistic attitude, etc. These become the common sense of the intellectuals and proletariats.

The philosophical syntheses of collectivism, entrepreneurship, communism, Christianism or love of others, service to the people, etc. are overpowered by the philosophical syntheses of individualism, competition, capitalism and neoliberalism, and that shaped the "*common sense*" and hypocritical (Hippocrates turned his back to God and deviated from the will of God) attitudes of all strata of a society.

171

The term *"common sense"* is used by Gramsci to mean the uncritical and largely unconscious way of perceiving and understanding the world that has become "common" in any given generational period, and an intellectual revolution is not performed by simply confronting one philosophical synthesis particularly neoliberalism with another philosophy like communism, Christianism or entrepreneurship. It is not just the ideas that require to be confronted but the social forces (bad religions, schools censoring philosophy, and curtailing academic freedom, tyrant government and her apparatuses, etc.) behind them and, more directly, the ideology these forces have generated and which has become part of what Gramsci calls "common sense". Individual values that prevails nowadays and the government and institutional culture hinders entrepreneurship.

In acquiring one's conception of the world one always belongs to a particular grouping which is that of all the social elements which share the same mode of thinking and acting. We are all *"conformists"* of some conformism or other, always man-in-the- mass or collective man.

Accordingly, the term 'conformity' does not mean for Gramsci as the negative tendency of people to let themselves be driven and conditioned by 'fashion', but rather an instrument for the interpretation of the process through which the majority of the population, within any society and under any regime, usually follows tradition and sticks to the regulations:

> "Conformity, then, means nothing other than 'sociality', but it is nice to use the word 'conformity' precisely because it annoys imbeciles. [...] It is too easy to be original simply by doing the opposite of what everyone else is doing [...]. What is really difficult is to put the stress on discipline and sociality and still profess sincerity, spontaneity, originality and personality."

Gramsci (in Hoare and Smith, 1971) when one's conception of the world is not critical and coherent but disjointed and episodic, one belongs simultaneously to a multiplicity of mass human groups. "Every social group, coming into existence on the original terrain of an essential function in the world of economic production, creates organically, together with itself, one or more strata of intellectuals which give it homogeneity and an awareness of its own function not only in the economic but also in the

173

social and political fields."

The central message of Gramsci is that the organization of culture is 'organic' to the dominant power. Intellectuals cannot be defined as such by the job they do, but rather by the role they play within society; this function is always, more or less consciously, that of the technical and political 'leadership' of a group, either the dominant group or another, tending towards a dominant position. Organisational leaders are commonly power hungry and the cultures within the egalitarian or social organisations which are part of their individual values immediately perished as they climb to the next power ladder like political election and or appointment. Opportunism overshadowed the values of organic intellectual or entrepreneur.

The entrepreneur him/herself represents a higher level of social organization, already characterized by a certain managerial and technical (i.e. intellectual) capacity. He or she must be organic upon completion of his/her mission of economic development; and must look and leave for other poor organisation or community.

These tendencies however are not just the barriers for entrepreneurial success. We have evaluated, analysed and criticised ourselves---intellectuals and proletariats. We have found and experienced working with others who are disillusioned by the "apparatuses" of the government by keeping the status quo and serve and preserve the neoliberal interests of economic expansion and accumulation of profit and wealth along with their (government officials) interest to perpetually remain in corrupt power.

I have personally experienced the coercive power of and injustices in the hands of the Philippines courts, LGU's, Commission on Human Rights, Philippines National Police, Securities and Exchange Commissions, Cooperative Development Authority, Office of the Ombudsman. I have experienced also the tyranny of U.S. FinCEN, Federal Bureau of Investigation, and International Monetary Fund. They created similar systems to legally discriminate and destroy anyone who opposed neoliberalism or in promotion of collectivism.

Conclusion

Individualism or any self-interest-driven undertaking or self-profiteering is not Entrepreneurship. Neither the individuals who performs economic function and without due consideration to social aspects of other people are entrepreneurs.

Entrepreneurship is not for individual personal enrichment but for all members of an organisation or community. An Entrepreneur never fades upon receipt of death threats in any forms, nor upon disapproval of the majority, does not conform to the common sense, but firmly believes in his or her social and economic functions.

Entrepreneurship must be accurately viewed as a solution to economic stagnation (opposite of economic development).

In Christian teachings, it is "let no man seek his own, but every man another's wealth." (I Corinthians 10:24). To rephrase this in active form, every true Christian must say and do this to one another; **"I will help you become rich,"** otherwise everyone is Satan's in disguise of Christ's.

References

1. Agustin, R.C. (2009) *Christian Communism*, ((published an excerpt to Wikipedia but censored and deleted without the author's prior knowledge. Presently under revision for publication).

2. AJ. (2015) *Gordon W. Allport's Trait Theory.* http://ajwrites57.hubpages.com/hub/Cardinal-Traits-Psychology

3. Anthony RN (1965) *Planning and Control Systems: A Framework for Analysis.* Harvard Business School Division of Research, Boston.

4. Avolio, B., Waldman, D., & Yammarino, F. (1991) *Leading in the 1990's: The four I's of Transformational Leadership. Journal of European Industrial Training.*

5. Baier, Horst, Lepsius, R, Mommsen, W., et, al. (Ed) (2001) *Economy and Society. Max Weber Gesamtausgabe (Collected Works)* Tübingen, Germany: J. C. B. Mohr & Paul Siebeck.

6. Bass, B., & Steidlmeier, P. (1999) *Ethics, Character, and Transformational Leadership Behavior.The Leadership Quarterly.*

7. Beardwell, J. and Claydon, T. (2007) *Human Resource Management: A Contemporary Approach.* 5th ed. Harlow: Prentice Hall.

8. Bowdon, Tom Butler*50 Prosperity Classics: Attract It, Create It, and Manage It, Share It*. London & Boston: Nicholas Brealey.

9. Burns, J. M. (1978) *Leadership*. New York: Harper & Row.

10. Caballero, R. (2014) *Creative Destruction.* http://economics.mit.edu/files/1785

11. Carless, S. A., Wearing, A. J., & Mann, L. (2000) *A short measure of transformational leadership. Journal of Business and Psychology.*

12. Challis P. & Challis L. (2014) *The Heat of Corporate Social Responsibility* (1st Ed.). London: Bookboom.com

13. Chan Kim W and Renee Mauborgne (2004) *Blue Ocean Strategy*. Harvard Business Review. MA: Harvard Press

14. Cherry, K. (2015) *What Are Cardinal Traits?* http://psychology.about.com/od/cindex/g/cardinaltraits .htm

15. Clarke, S. (1991) *The Neoliberal Theory of Society.* https://homepages.warwick.ac.uk/~syrbe/pubs/Neolib eralism.pdf

16. Copeland, M.K. (2014) *the emerging significance of Values Based Leadership: A Literature Review. International Journal of Leadership Studies*, Vol. 8 Iss. 2, 2014. USA: Regent University

17. DiMaggio and Powell, (1991) The *New Institutionalism in Organizational Analysis*. Chicago: University of Chicago Press.

18. Dobbin, F. (1994) *Economic Sociology*. USA: Harvard Press. http://scholar.harvard.edu/files/dobbin/files/

19. Drucker, P. F. (1985) *Innovation and Entrepreneurship. Practice and Principles*, New York: Harper & Row.

20. Drucker, P. *Drucker's Life & legacy*.
http://www.druckerinstitute.com/peter-druckers-life-and-legacy/

21. Elliot, J. (1980) *Marx and Schumpeter on Capitalism's Creative Destruction: A Comparative Restatements*. The Quarterly Journal of Economics.Vol. 95. USA: MIT Press.

22. Friedman, M & Friedman, R. (1962) *Capitalism and Freedom*. Chicago: Chicago University Press.

23. Friedman, Milton (1970) *The Social Responsibility of Business is to Increase Its Profit*. New York: New York Times Co.

24. Gilligan, C. (1982) *In A Different Voice*. MA: Harvard University Press.

25. _____ (1993) *Theory of Moral Development*.
http://education-portal.com/academy/lesson/carol-gilligans-theory-of-moral-development.html

26. Gramsci, A. Edited by Hoare and Smith (1999) *Prison Notebooks*. London

27. Gramsci, A. (1971) Edited by Quintin Hoare and Geoffrey Nowell-Smith *Selections from the Prison Notebooks*. London

28. Grebel. T, Pyka, A. & Hanusch, H. (2003) An Evolutionary Approach to the Theory of the Entrepreneur. USA: Edward Elgar.

29. Hofstede, G.H. (1968) The Game of Budget Control. Tavistock, London

30. Investopedia. http://www.investopdeia.com

31. Hayek, F., [1990] (1946) 'The Meaning of Competition' in Stephen Littlechild (editor), *Austrian Economics*, volume III, Brookfield, Vermont, Edward Elgar.

32. Hebert, & Link, (2009) A History of Entrepreneurship. USA: Taylor & Francis.

33. Kim, Sung Ho. (2012) "Max Weber", *The Stanford Encyclopaedia of Philosophy* (Fall 2012 Edition), and Edward N. Zalta (ed.). http://plato.stanford.edu/archives/fall2012/entries/weber/

34. Kirzner, Israel M. (1973). Competition and entrepreneurship. Chicago: University of Chicago Press.

35. Klimsza, & Lucjan. (2014). *Business Ethics: Introduction to the Ethics of Values*. Bookboon.com.

36. Kondoh, S., N. Mishima, Y. Hotta, K. Watari, T. Kurita and K. Masui. (2008) *Evaluation and Re-design Method of Manufacturing Processes.* Japan: National Institute for Advanced Industrial Science and Technology

37. Knowles, G. (2011). *Quality Management.* Bookboon.com

38. Leonard, Thomas C. (2007) *Redeemed By History.* University A review essay on Prophet of Innovation: Joseph Schumpeter and Creative Destruction of T. McCraw. Department of Economics Princeton, Cambridge, MA: Harvard University Press.

39. Lowe EA (1971) *On the Idea of a Management Control System: Integrating Accounting and Management Control*. London Manage.

40. Lowe EA, Machin JLJ (eds) (1983) *New Perspectives in Management Control*. London: Macmillan.

41. Lowe, K., Kroeck, K., & Sivasubramaniam, N. (1996) *Effectiveness Correlates of Transformational and Transactional Leadership: A meta- review of the MLQLiterature.The Leadership Quarterly*.

42. Lucas 1978, Evans and Jovanovic 1989, Murphy et al. (1991) *Economic Theory. Entrepreneurship*

43. Marx, K. (1973) Trans. by Nicolaus, M. *Grundrisse.* Penguin.

44. Monasta, Attilio. (2000). *Antonio Gramsci*. Paris, UNESCO: International Bureau of Education.

45. Mullins, L.J. (2005). *Management and Organization Behaviour*. (7th edition). England: Harlow.

46. Naudé, Wim. (2013). *Entrepreneurship and Economic Development: Theory, Evidence and Policy*. Germany: IZA

47. Pittaway, Dr. Luke William & A. Freeman (2011) .*The Evolution of Entrepreneurship Theory*. USA: GSU.

48. Quin, S. (2010). *Management Basics.* 1st Ed. Bookboon.com.

49. Rathe AW (1960) *Management Control in Business. In: Malcolm DJ, Rowe AJ (eds) Management control systems*. Wiley, New York

50. Rawls, John (1971). *A Theory of Justice*. Mass: Harvard University Press.

51. Salmon Valley Business & Innovation Center. http://www.svbic.com/node/24

52. Schumpeter, J. A. (1939) *Business Cycles: A Theoretical, Historical, and Statistical Analysis of the Capitalist Process*, McGraw-Hill Book Company Inc., New York

53. Schumpeter, J.A. (1950) *Capitalism, Socialism and Democracy*. New York: Harper.

54. Schumpeter, J.A. (1961) *The Theory of Economic Development*. New York: Oxford. 1961.

55. Schumpeter, J.A. (1971) edited by Peter Kilby. Entrepreneurship and economic development. New York: Free Press.

56. Sheperd, Peter. 2015. *Moral Development*. http://www.trans4mind.com/heart/tools07.html

57. Walzer, M. (1983). *Sphere of Justice: A Defense of Pluralism and Equality*. USA:Basic Books

58. Weber, Max. 1919/1946. *"Science as a Vocation" in From Max Weber.*

59. ——, 1920/1946. *"The Protestant Sects and the Spirit of Capitalism"*

60. Weinbach, R.W. (1994). *The Social Worker as a Manager: Theory and Practice*. (2nd edition). Boston: Allyn & Bacon.

ABOUT THE AUTHOR

Rannie C. Agustin, a servant of Christ and a communist,
is a former college Instructor to Management and Economics and
presently a management and investment consultant, and the
chairman-owner of rania Child Development Center.

Email: raniagustin@yahoo.com

twitter@raniagustin

COMING SOON!

The Volume 2 of this book will discuss the Change management; case study as a requirement to study social and or economic phenomena for the formulation of alternative courses of action and models. The alternatives are to be assessed with feasibility study. A very important chapter and part of Feasibility Study Preparation is the Situation Analysis and the Historical perspective of project location.

In this book, the author will discuss among others the managerial analysis of the failure of comrades to let the workers run the affairs of Union Soviet made by Leon Trotsky, the desperate measures taken by elders of Kibbutz in Israel, the failures of some cadres in Chinese collective communities after Mao's death and failures of Philippines *bayanihan* and collective communities from the hands of Spaniards and Americans.

The change management, case (phenomena/incidents) study and feasibility study preparations are parts of the Volume 2 titled: **"Entrepreneurship: The Planning Phase."**

www.ingramcontent.com/pod-product-compliance
Lightning Source LLC
Chambersburg PA
CBHW051909170526
45168CB00001B/310